Teenage Sexuality

Other Books of Related Interest:

Opposing Viewpoints Series

Children and the Entertainment Industry

Sexually Transmitted Diseases

Teen Drug Abuse

At Issue Series

Age of Consent

Do Abstinence Programs Work

Is Childhood Becoming Too Sexualized

Current Controversies Series

Teens and Privacy

Teen Pregnancy and Parenting

"Congress shall make no law ... abridging the freedom of speech, or of the press."

First Amendment to the US Constitution

The basic foundation of our democracy is the First Amendment guarantee of freedom of expression. The Opposing Viewpoints Series is dedicated to the concept of this basic freedom and the idea that it is more important to practice it than to enshrine it.

Teenage Sexuality

Aarti D. Stephens, Book Editor

GREENHAVEN PRESS
A part of Gale, Cengage Learning

Detroit • New York • San Francisco • New Haven, Conn • Waterville, Maine • London

Elizabeth Des Chenes, *Managing Editor*

For more information, contact:
Greenhaven Press
27500 Drake Rd.
Farmington Hills, MI 48331-3535
Or you can visit our Internet site at gale.cengage.com

For product information and technology assistance, contact us at

Gale Customer Support, 1-800-877-4253
For permission to use material from this text or product, submit all requests online at
www.cengage.com/permissions

Further permissions questions can be emailed to permissionrequest@cengage.com

Articles in Greenhaven Press anthologies are often edited for length to meet page requirements. In addition, original titles of these works are changed to clearly present the main thesis and to explicitly indicate the author's opinion. Every effort is made to ensure that Greenhaven Press accurately reflects the original intent of the authors. Every effort has been made to trace the owners of copyrighted material.

Cover image © Johner Images/Alamy.

LIBRARY OF CONGRESS CATALOGING-IN-PUBLICATION DATA

Teenage sexuality / Aarti D. Stephens, book editor.
    p. cm. -- (Opposing viewpoints)
Summary: "Teenage Sexuality: What Factors Influence Teenage Sexuality?; What Are Some Significant Teen Sexuality Issues?; How Should Society Educate Teens About Sex?; How Should Society Respond to Teenage Sexuality?"-- Provided by publisher.
    Includes bibliographical references and index.
    ISBN 978-0-7377-5763-7 (hardback) -- ISBN 978-0-7377-5764-4 (pbk.)
    1. Teenagers--Sexual behavior--United States. 2. Teenagers--United States--Attitudes. 3. Teenage pregnancy--United States. 4. Sex instruction for teenagers--United States. 5. Homosexuality--United States. I. I. Stephens, Aarti D.
    HQ27.T378 2012
    306.708350973--dc23

                                      2011038893

Printed in Mexico

Contents

Chapter 3: How Should Society Educate Teens About Sex?

Chapter 4: How Should Society Respond to Teenage Sexuality?

Why Consider Opposing Viewpoints?

> *"The only way in which a human being can make some approach to knowing the whole of a subject is by hearing what can be said about it by persons of every variety of opinion and studying all modes in which it can be looked at by every character of mind. No wise man ever acquired his wisdom in any mode but this."*
>
> *John Stuart Mill*

In our media-intensive culture it is not difficult to find differing opinions. Thousands of newspapers and magazines and dozens of radio and television talk shows resound with differing points of view. The difficulty lies in deciding which opinion to agree with and which "experts" seem the most credible. The more inundated we become with differing opinions and claims, the more essential it is to hone critical reading and thinking skills to evaluate these ideas. Opposing Viewpoints books address this problem directly by presenting stimulating debates that can be used to enhance and teach these skills. The varied opinions contained in each book examine many different aspects of a single issue. While examining these conveniently edited opposing views, readers can develop critical thinking skills such as the ability to compare and contrast authors' credibility, facts, argumentation styles, use of persuasive techniques, and other stylistic tools. In short, the Opposing Viewpoints Series is an ideal way to attain the higher-level thinking and reading skills so essential in a culture of diverse and contradictory opinions.

In addition to providing a tool for critical thinking, Opposing Viewpoints books challenge readers to question their own strongly held opinions and assumptions. Most people form their opinions on the basis of upbringing, peer pressure, and personal, cultural, or professional bias. By reading carefully balanced opposing views, readers must directly confront new ideas as well as the opinions of those with whom they disagree. This is not to simplistically argue that everyone who reads opposing views will—or should—change his or her opinion. Instead, the series enhances readers' understanding of their own views by encouraging confrontation with opposing ideas. Careful examination of others' views can lead to the readers' understanding of the logical inconsistencies in their own opinions, perspective on why they hold an opinion, and the consideration of the possibility that their opinion requires further evaluation.

Evaluating Other Opinions

To ensure that this type of examination occurs, Opposing Viewpoints books present all types of opinions. Prominent spokespeople on different sides of each issue as well as well-known professionals from many disciplines challenge the reader. An additional goal of the series is to provide a forum for other, less known, or even unpopular viewpoints. The opinion of an ordinary person who has had to make the decision to cut off life support from a terminally ill relative, for example, may be just as valuable and provide just as much insight as a medical ethicist's professional opinion. The editors have two additional purposes in including these less known views. One, the editors encourage readers to respect others' opinions—even when not enhanced by professional credibility. It is only by reading or listening to and objectively evaluating others' ideas that one can determine whether they are worthy of consideration. Two, the inclusion of such viewpoints encourages the important critical thinking skill of objectively evaluating an author's credentials and bias. This evaluation will illuminate an author's reasons for taking a particular stance on an issue and will aid in readers' evaluation of the author's ideas.

It is our hope that these books will give readers a deeper understanding of the issues debated and an appreciation of the complexity of even seemingly simple issues when good and honest people disagree. This awareness is particularly important in a democratic society such as ours in which people enter into public debate to determine the common good. Those with whom one disagrees should not be regarded as enemies but rather as people whose views deserve careful examination and may shed light on one's own.

Thomas Jefferson once said that "difference of opinion leads to inquiry, and inquiry to truth." Jefferson, a broadly educated man, argued that "if a nation expects to be ignorant and free . . . it expects what never was and never will be." As individuals and as a nation, it is imperative that we consider the opinions of others and examine them with skill and discernment. The Opposing Viewpoints Series is intended to help readers achieve this goal.

David L. Bender and Bruno Leone,
Founders

Introduction

"How sexuality, love, and autonomy are perceived and negotiated in parent-child relationships and among teenagers depends on the cultural templates people have available."

Amy Schalet, 2010

Teenage years are a unique confluence of physical, emotional, and social changes in the lives of young adults. New bodies, new environments, and a heightened sense and awareness of their peers are only some of the issues teens grapple with as they begin their first significant, independent foray into the world. This transition from teen to adult begins in middle school and continues through high school and early college years. For many teens, these years are their first opportunity to begin operating independently of direct parental or adult supervision. This newfound freedom is accompanied by significant physical and emotional changes for teens, and one of the most significant among these is learning to navigate their own sexuality.

Teen sexuality has been a hot-button issue for many decades, but it did not gain center stage in American public policy and education debates until the 1970s, when sexuality began to be addressed more openly in society. At that time, American discourse about sexuality was very conservative when it came to teens. Attitudes in the United States have liberalized somewhat since then, though commentators have pointed out that they remain conservative relative to attitudes in some European countries. Even though the United States and Europe traversed the road to sexual liberalization on almost parallel paths, American teens experience adolescent sex much differently than their European counterparts.

This difference is highlighted by Amy Schalet in her article titled "Sex, Love, and Autonomy in the Teenage Sleepover," published in *Contexts* in 2010. In her report comparing American parental attitudes toward teen sexuality versus their Dutch counterparts, Schalet cites the example of Karel Doorman, whose daughter, Heidi, is almost seventeen years old. Although Doorman keeps tabs on his daughter's computer use and is an involved parent who makes sure that Heidi is on track with her school performance, he does not object to the idea of his daughter having a sexual relationship. In fact, Doorman told Schalet that he is open to Heidi having her current boyfriend spend the night at their house, and he went on to observe that he actually suspects that his daughter "might prefer a partner of her own sex." Doorman's approach is in stark contrast to California native Rhonda Fursman, also interviewed by Schalet, who told her teenage children that "premarital sex . . . is on the list with shoplifting . . . sort of like the Ten Commandments: don't do any of those because if you do, you're going to be in a world of hurt."

The difference between Doorman's and Fursman's approaches and attitudes highlights one of the biggest unresolved issues about teenage sexuality in America today. Even though a majority of American adolescents will, like their peers in the Netherlands and much of industrialized Europe, engage in sexual relationships before they exit their teen years, sexual activity among teens is widely viewed as a negative in the United States. Despite the abundance of surveys demonstrating premarital sexual relationships among adults as the norm, adolescent sexual behavior in the United States is almost always regarded as unacceptable. Schalet theorizes that this is so because teen sexual behavior in America is linked to its unintended consequences, such as pregnancy and sexually transmitted diseases. The United States had the highest rate of teen pregnancy among industrialized nations during the 1970s and 1980s, and although these numbers have dropped somewhat, teen pregnancies and other negative teen sexual health outcomes in America still rank high compared to other developed nations. These trends contribute to American ambivalence and confusion about teenage sex and complicate issues surrounding the dissemination of information. Americans continue to heatedly debate teenage sexuality with little consensus, leaving many issues unresolved and unaddressed.

In contrast, notes Schalet, evolving attitudes about sexuality in the Netherlands resulted in acceptance of sexuality, even teen sexuality, as healthy and normal. These changing attitudes were accompanied by health policies adapted to reflect the sexual behavior of their populations. Sexuality was viewed as private and personal, and health policies in the Netherlands supported this premise, with the goal of providing resources that aided in enhancing health outcomes. Eventually, this methodology was applied to teens, providing for equal and open access to information and resources that addressed sexual issues faced by young people. Within the context of the larger discussion about sexuality, Dutch society has removed many emotional barriers around teen sexuality, viewing it as a normal and expected step toward adulthood. American society, however, continues to struggle when it comes to teens and sex, and this conflict is most vividly reflected in the debate surrounding American sex-education programs. Sex education in the United States has tended to emphasize abstinence only until marriage, though some programs do offer comprehensive sex education, including discussions of condoms and other contraceptives. In the meantime, American teenagers struggle to deal with sexual choices that they are often forced to make in an atmosphere of intense peer pressure and under a host of biological and emotional influences they are ill-equipped to handle.

In the viewpoints that follow, sociologists, medical practitioners, researchers, commentators, and journalists offer varying opinions on teenage sexuality in four chapters: What Factors Influence Teenage Sexuality?, What Are Some Significant Teen Sexuality Issues?, How Should Society Educate Teens About Sex?, and How Should Society Respond to Teenage Sexuality? The varying positions expressed in *Opposing Viewpoints: Teenage Sexuality* convey the complexity, sensitivity, and difficulty of the issues surrounding teenage sexuality.

OPPOSING
VIEWPOINTS®
SERIES

 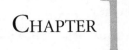

What Factors Influence Teenage Sexuality?

Chapter Preface

One-third of high school students taking the SAT in 2011 received the following question as their prompt for the essay portion of the test:

> Reality-television programs, which feature real people engaged in real activities rather than professional actors performing scripted scenes, are increasingly popular. These shows depict ordinary people competing in everything from singing and dancing to losing weight, or just living their everyday lives. Most people believe that the reality these shows portray is authentic, but they are being misled. . . . Do people benefit from forms of entertainment that show so-called reality, or are such forms of entertainment harmful?

The question sparked controversy because many parents and students felt that it placed at a disadvantage those students who do not watch reality television. Teens who had avoided such programs because they considered them harmful or a waste of time felt that the inclusion of this particular writing prompt on the SAT legitimized reality television and its place in contemporary culture.

There is growing concern among parents and educators about the impact of reality television shows, specifically those marketed to teens. The biggest culprits, according to many parenting groups and media analysts, are reality shows featuring romantic relationships, many of which include significant sexual content. Two of the most-cited examples of this type of programming are *Teen Mom* and *The Bachelor*, shows that are among the most-watched programs by teen audiences.

Concern about the impact of reality television on teen sexuality is supported by a Rand Corporation study, released in November 2008, which revealed that adolescents who watch television loaded with sexual content are twice as likely to get pregnant or impregnate someone else. The American Academy of Pediatrics (AAP) concurs, noting on its website that "the media may act as a 'superpeer' in convincing adolescents that sexual activity is normative behavior for young teenagers." Discussing the issue of media influence on teens in an article on DailyFinance.com, Sarah Gilbert wrote, "Sex sells, it always has, and it sells particularly well to those who don't know any better: . . . kids." The Rand Corporation's study estimates that an average American teenager watches television three hours a day and much of the programming they view contains "heavy doses of sexual content, ranging from touching, kissing, jokes, and innuendo to conversations about sexual activity and portrayals of intercourse." Sex on reality television shows in particular is often presented as a casual activity, with no risk or consequences.

The findings of the study reflect concerns that researchers and psychologists have expressed about the pervasiveness of sexual content in media directed toward teens, especially in shows like *Teen Mom* and *16 and Pregnant*. What complicates the situation even further is that the kids featured on these shows have become celebrities—many of them have an online media presence, including Twitter accounts and Facebook pages that their teen fans follow avidly. In a society that reveres celebrity, and where celebrities serve as role models, many parents are concerned about the example set by reality television stars. Even though the stated intent of these shows is to highlight the negative consequences of unprotected sex, the fame achieved by the people on these shows makes it appear as if there is no downside to the sexual choices they make. *Teen Mom* is sponsored by The National Campaign to Prevent Teen and Unplanned Pregnancy, which has argued that any attention to the issue of teen pregnancy is a good thing. However, critics note that the situations highlighted in these shows do not focus on contraception and prevention, but instead on the melodrama associated with pregnancy, often concluding the stories with neat, happy endings.

Even though teens get sexuality information from many sources, televised portrayals of relationships are a strong influence on teen perceptions about sexuality, including their sense of what is normal and what is not. According to a Harris Interactive survey conducted in 2007, 68 percent of television shows have explicit sexual content, while only 15 percent discuss risks and consequences. Many parents and social commentators have expressed concern about the negative impact on young people when television shows aimed at teens fail to portray balanced, healthy relationships and gloss over the risks associated with sex.

Television shows are but one influence on teens. The viewpoints in the chapter that follows highlight several influences on teens, debating the role and impact of other factors on teenage sexuality.

> *"Research confirms what many of us know instinctively: that parents can be one of the strongest influences in adolescents' lives."*

Parents Are a Strong Influence on Teenage Sexuality

Erum Ikramullah, Jennifer Manlove, Carol Cui, and Kristin A. Moore

Child Trends is a nonprofit, nonpartisan organization that researches children at all developmental stages. Erum Ikramullah is a senior research analyst there; Jennifer Manlove is the program area director and senior research scientist; Carol Cui is a research scholar; and Kristin A. Moore is a senior scholar and senior program area co-director. In the following viewpoint, the authors present research that demonstrates the strong influence of parents on adolescent behavior, including sexual activity. They conclude that parenting practices put in place prior to adolescent sexual activity—such as communication, monitoring, and daily routines that include family time—have a significant impact on delaying sex among teens.

As you read, consider the following questions:

1. According to the authors, what percentage of teens report their parents as having the most influence on their decisions regarding sex?

2. What are two important steps parents can take to help prevent risky teenage behavior?

3. What specific benefits result from establishing family routines in helping adolescents make decisions about their sexual experiences?

Adolescents are influenced by a variety of social factors and institutions. Prior research confirms what many of us know instinctively: that parents can be one of the strongest influences in adolescents' lives. For example, higher levels of parental involvement in their adolescents' lives are linked with lower levels of delinquency, violent behavior, high-school dropout, and drug abuse, as well as with higher levels of educational attainment. In this *Research Brief*, we look specifically at whether parental involvement in adolescence reduces the chances of teens being sexually active at a young age.

Compelling reasons exist for exploring this topic. Early adolescent sexual experience is linked with a variety of risky outcomes, including acquiring a sexually transmitted infection (STI) and having an unintended pregnancy. Because of the significant role that parents can potentially play in influencing their teens to delay having sex—thus reducing the risk of negative reproductive health outcomes—it is important to understand whether and how multiple dimensions of parental involvement are associated with the timing of teens' first sexual experience.

To further this understanding, Child Trends analyzed data from the National Longitudinal Survey of Youth—1997 [NLSY97] cohort to explore how parenting practices that occur before adolescents become sexually experienced are associated with the probability of sexual experience by age 16. This *Research Brief* reports our key findings. We found that multiple measures of parental involvement and engagement are associated with delayed sex among teens. These measures include positive parent-adolescent relationship quality, high parental awareness and monitoring, and family dinner routines. Specifically, our analyses showed that adolescent girls who reported higher quality relationships with their mothers and fathers, and adolescent boys who reported that they ate dinner with their families every day were less likely to have sexual intercourse at an early age. The same held true for both adolescent girls and adolescent boys who reported that their parents kept close tabs on whom they were with when not at home.

Parents' Influence on Adolescent Sexual Activity

In two recent nationally representative polls of 12- to 19-year-olds and of adults aged 20 and older (including parents of teens), respondents were asked about who they think is most influential when it comes to teens' decisions about sex. Response categories included: parents, friends, teachers and sex educators, religious leaders, the media, siblings, teens themselves, or someone else.

Parents have more influence than they think on their adolescents' decisions about sex. Nearly one-half of 12- to 19-year-olds (47 percent) reported that their parents had the most influence on their decisions about sex. However, only one-third of parents of adolescents (34 percent) reported that parents were the most influential. Parents most frequently cited adolescents' friends as having the most influence on their adolescent children's decisions about sex (41 percent).

Fifty-nine percent of 12- to 14-year-olds and 39 percent of 15- to 19-year-olds reported that parents had the most influence on their decisions about sex, compared with 34 percent of parents of adolescents of all ages (data for parents are not available by specific ages of their adolescent children).

Parent-Adolescent Relationship Quality

Although some previous studies have found an association between better parent-adolescent relationships and delayed sexual initiation among adolescents, limited research exists that specifically examines both mother-adolescent and father-adolescent relationships. In the NLSY97, adolescents reported on their relationship quality with each parent by level of agreement with the following statements: "I think highly of parent," "I enjoy spending time with parent," and "Parent is a person I want to be like." In our analyses, we categorized responses to these statements as representing low, medium, and high levels of relationship quality.

Adolescent girls report better relationships with their mothers, on average, compared with adolescent boys, while adolescent boys tend to report better relationships with their fathers than do adolescent girls. Forty percent of adolescent girls reported high relationship quality with their mothers, compared with 31 percent of adolescent boys. On the other hand, 40 percent of adolescent boys reported high relationship quality with their fathers, compared with 34 percent of adolescent girls.

Among adolescent girls living with two residential parents, about one in four (24 percent) reported high relationship quality with both parents, compared with about one in 10 (11 percent) who reported low relationship quality with both parents. Findings were similar for adolescent boys.

Higher levels of parent-adolescent relationship quality are associated with reduced risk of early sexual experience among teen girls, even after taking account of other background factors. Teen girls who reported higher levels of relationship quality with their mothers were less likely to have sex before age 16 (an estimated 25 percent and 26 percent for high and medium levels, respectively), compared with teen girls who reported poorer relationships with their mothers (an estimated 36 percent).

Additionally, teen girls who reported higher levels of relationship quality with their fathers were less likely to have sex before age 16 (21 percent and 23 percent for high and medium levels, respectively), compared with teen girls who reported lower levels of father-daughter relationship quality (31 percent).

No significant association was found between parent-adolescent relationship quality and early sexual experience among teen boys.

Positive relationships with both parents in adolescence are associated with lower levels of early sexual activity among teen girls. Specifically, among teen girls who lived with two residential parents, those who reported high relationship quality with both parents were less likely to have sex at an early age (22 percent), compared with teen girls who reported low relationship quality with both parents (37 percent).

No significant association was found for teen boys on this measure.

Parental Awareness and Monitoring

Parents can help prevent risky teen behavior by monitoring their adolescents' activities and being aware of where and with whom their adolescents are when they are not at home or in school. We measured parental awareness and monitoring about their adolescents based on the following question asked of adolescents: "How much does he/she know about who you are with when you are not at home?" Adolescents could respond that their parent knows: everything, most things, some things, just a little, or nothing. Adolescents reported on both maternal and paternal awareness. We also created a measure of parental awareness and monitoring based on the average awareness and monitoring responses of the mother and father.

Adolescent girls report higher levels of parental awareness and monitoring than do adolescent boys. Forty-three percent of adolescent girls reported their parent (or parents) knows everything about whom they are with when not at home, compared with 32 percent of adolescent boys.

Adolescent girls reported higher levels of both maternal and paternal awareness than did adolescent boys (47 percent versus 35 percent when it came to maternal awareness and 30 percent versus 24 percent when it came to paternal awareness).

Teens of both sexes who report higher levels of parental awareness were less likely to have had sexual intercourse before age 16, even when controlling for other background characteristics. Teen girls with higher levels of parental, maternal, and paternal awareness were less likely to have initiated sex before age 16. Less than one-quarter of teen girls (22 percent) who reported that their parent or parents knew everything about whom they were with when not at home had sex before age 16, compared with 29 percent who reported that their parent or parents knew most things about whom they were with when not at home and 43 percent who reported that their parent or parents knew just some things or less about whom they were with when not at home.

Teen boys who reported the lowest levels (knows some things or less) of parental awareness were more likely to have had sex before age 16, compared with those who reported medium (knows most things) and high levels (knows everything) of awareness (43 percent, compared with 33 percent and 30 percent, respectively).

Separate analyses showed a similar pattern of association between maternal and paternal awareness and age at first sex for teen girls and teen boys.

Family Dinner Routines

Family routines—or time spent by parents and adolescents together—is another dimension of parental involvement that

Parents Are Influential

This graph reflects answers teens gave for a survey that asked: "When it comes to your decisions about sex, who is most influential?"

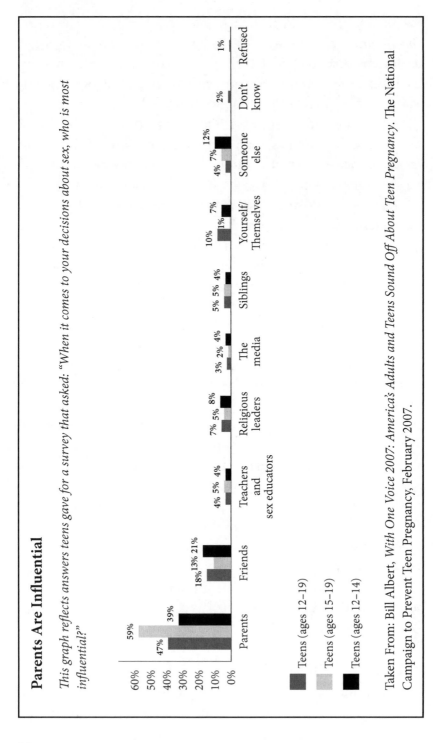

Teens (ages 12–19)

Teens (ages 15–19)

Teens (ages 12–14)

Taken From: Bill Albert, *With One Voice 2007: America's Adults and Teens Sound Off About Teen Pregnancy*. The National Campaign to Prevent Teen Pregnancy, February 2007.

may influence adolescent behaviors. The following section highlights our findings on the association between the number of days a week that adolescents have dinner with their family and their probability of sexual experience before age 16.

More than two-fifths of 12- to 14-year-olds report having dinner with their family every day. Boys in this age group reported having dinner more often with their families than did girls in this age group. Specifically, 46 percent of the boys reported having dinner with their family every day, compared with 41 percent of the girls.

Nearly one-third of adolescent girls (31 percent) reported having dinner with their families from zero to four days a week, compared with just one-quarter of adolescent boys.

Teen boys who report having dinner with their family every day were less likely to have had sex before age 16, compared with those who report they eat dinner with their family less than five nights a week, even after controlling for other background factors.

Thirty-one percent of teen boys who reported having dinner with their family every day were estimated to have had sex before age 16, compared with 37 percent of teen boys who reported that they had dinner with their family fewer than five days a week.

No significant association was found between family dinner routines and early sexual experience among teen girls.

Key Findings

This *Research Brief* has highlighted several dimensions of parental involvement in adolescents' lives, including parent-adolescent relationship quality, parental awareness and monitoring about whom their adolescents spend time with, and frequency of eating dinner together as a family. Our analyses assessed the association between levels of parental involvement and the probability of sexual intercourse before age 16 and highlight the role of parental involvement in delaying the timing of when teens first have sex. These findings support previous research showing an association between parental involvement and adolescent sexual behaviors. The following key findings and implications have emerged from our research:

Many adolescents themselves report that their parents have the most influence when it comes to their decisions about sex. More than one-half of 12- to 14-year-olds reported that their parents have the most influence on their decisions about sex. In contrast, only about one-third of parents of adolescents reported that parents have the most influence on their adolescents' decisions about sex. These findings underscore the need for parents to recognize the level of influence that they have and, thus, to develop positive parenting practices and healthy parent-adolescent relationships that may help to delay sexual activity among their teens.

Better parent-adolescent relationships are associated with a lower probability of sexual intercourse before age 16, among teen girls. This finding holds true for mother-adolescent, father-adolescent, and combined parent-adolescent relationship quality, showing that both mothers and fathers can have a positive influence on their teenage daughters' behaviors. Much research attention has been given to the role of mothers in this area. However, these findings, and those of other researchers, suggest that fathers may have just as important a role to play as mothers in helping their teenage daughters make responsible decisions about sex.

Adolescents whose parents are more aware of whom they are with when not at home are less likely to have sex by age 16. Again, this finding holds true for maternal, paternal, and overall parental awareness, signaling the importance of having at least one parent who is aware of the adolescent's friends and activities. Parents can help protect against risky sexual behaviors among their teenage children by getting to know their teens' friends and being aware of their teens' activities and whereabouts when they are not at home.

Teen boys who eat dinner with their family every day have a lower probability of having sex before age 16, compared with those who eat dinner with their family four days a week or less. Eating dinner together as a family represents one type of routine family activity. Programs designed to delay sexual activity and/or other risky behaviors can help improve outcomes for adolescents by encouraging them and their parents to engage in routine family interactions and activities. In addition, more family routines offer more opportunities for conversations between parents and children, possibly improving parent-teen communication. Although the association between routine family dinners and sexual experience before age 16 was not significant for teen girls, it is possible that their decisions about sex may be influenced by other types of family activity.

Programs designed to delay teen sexual activity and to deter other risky behaviors may benefit from including or enhancing parental involvement in their offerings. The analyses presented in this brief offer guidance to parents on ways that they can encourage their teens to delay sex and deter other risky behaviors. Our analyses also suggest steps that programs serving adolescents might take toward these ends. For example, our findings point to the value of adding a parental involvement component to sex education programs that do not currently engage parents. Currently, several sexual education programs do include parental involvement components. For such programs, the research suggests that such involvement should go beyond the typical discussions about the "sex talk" to a serious exploration of parenting practices associated with less sexual risk-taking by adolescents.

Parents Are a Critical Factor

Parental involvement in their adolescents' lives represents a critical factor associated with adolescent sexual behaviors. Our findings complement prior research, which has found that strong parent-adolescent relationship quality, communication, and monitoring and awareness of adolescents' activities are associated with delayed sexual initiation and a reduced risk of teen pregnancy.

Adolescents who feel close to their parents may be more comfortable communicating with their parents about sex, may share or feel more influenced by their parents' values, or may have a better understanding about their parents' expectation regarding their teens' sexual behaviors.

Recent data indicate a slight increase in sexual experience among teens, underscoring the importance of developing practices and programs that encourage teens to delay the initiation of sex or other risky sexual behaviors until they are older, thereby helping to reduce the number of unintended pregnancies and STIs among teens. The findings presented in this brief also suggest several simple and affordable parenting practices that can help strengthen families and improve adolescent outcomes.

"... in the real world teenagers' behaviour is shaped by the sort of peer pressure displayed during the sessions."

Peer Pressure Is a Strong Influence on Teenage Sexuality

Mark Hayter and Christina Harrison

Dr. Mark Hayter is a nurse educator and researcher with a focus on child and adolescent health and the promotion of healthy lifestyles among young people. Christina Harrison is a sexual health specialist nurse. Their research concludes that health professionals need to address all the factors that relate to teenage sexuality, including gender attitudes, alcohol, and peer pressure. Teens not only need to be well informed and prepared, but health professionals need to offer advice and support for these other factors involved.

As you read, consider the following questions:

1. According to the article, do male and female views of sexuality differ?

Mark Hayter and Christina Harrison, "Gendered Attitudes Towards Sexual Relationships Among Adolescents Attending Nurse Led Sexual Health Clinics in England: A Qualitative Study," *Journal of Clinical Nursing*, Wiley-Blackwell, vol. 17, November 2008, pp. 2963–71. Copyright © 2008, John Wiley and Sons. Reproduced by permission of Wiley-Blackwell Publishers.

2. As stated in the article, what should nurses do when it comes to female clients?

3. Should alcohol education be integrated into teenagers' sexual education according to the following viewpoint?

Alcohol and attitudes are two of the key factors that health professionals need to be aware of when they are dealing with sexually active teenagers.

Researchers from the University of Sheffield, UK, found considerable differences between the way that boys and girls aged 14 to 16 viewed a series of sexual scenarios.

"The girls who took part in our focus groups were more likely to see their partner's point of view and were more aware of the complex nature of relationships than the boys" says nurse researcher Dr Mark Hayter.

The Study

Ten focus groups were held with 35 teenagers who had accessed nurse-led sexual health outreach clinics for contraception. These clinics are often held in conjunction with youth clubs in areas where teenage pregnancy rates are high.

The participants were presented with a series of scenarios: a girl and a boy both reluctant to have sex, a girl who had had a numbers of partners and a girl who felt pressured to have sex because her friends had paired off with two boys leaving her with a third.

"The objective of this study was to explore the broad gender-based attitudes and opinions towards all of the case studies, not just to explore any differences between attitudes towards any one particular case study" explains Dr Hayter, who carried out the research with Christina Harrison, a sexual health specialist nurse from Doncaster Primary Care Trust.

"Male and female attitudes clearly differed. The girls' responses were more empathic and complex because they face more complex social pressures when it comes to having sex.

Teens Refer to Risky Behavior Online

Risk Behavior Referenced	Profiles With This Display (%)
Sexual Behavior	
Profiles with any references to sex	24.0
Profiles with self-disclosure of sexual activity	3.6
Substance Use	
Profiles with references to alcohol use	37.0
Profiles with references to tobacco use	13.0
Profiles with references to drug use	10.2
Profiles with references to use of any substance	41.0
Profiles with references to use of >1 substance	15.6
Profiles with references to use of all 3 substances	3.6
Violence	
Profiles with references to violence	14.4
Profiles with references to any of these 3 risk behaviors	54.4

Taken from: Megan A. Moreno et al., "Display of Health Risk Behaviors on MySpace By Adolescents," *Archives of Pediatrics & Adolescent Medicine*, January 2009.

The young men on the other hand appeared to follow behaviour patterns that included pressuring girls to have sex, often with the use of alcohol.

"We also noticed that the boys often used aggressive language about relationships—an element that was missing from the girls' focus groups. For example they suggested that a girlfriend who slept around would probably pay a physical price and that using tactics like getting a girl drunk were acceptable.

"In one of the boys' focus groups there was even a suggestion that it was OK for a boy to force his girlfriend to have sex and the group started trying to differentiate between 'just a bit of pressure' and 'proper rape.'"

Influences, Including Peer Pressure

The researchers concede that the focus group format could have encouraged stereotypical male and female behaviour, but point out that in the real world teenagers' behaviour is shaped by the sort of peer pressure displayed during the sessions.

Sexual health is a major issue in all cultures, with increasing numbers of young people between 13 and 18 being affected by sexually transmitted infections (STIs), unplanned pregnancies and abortions.

"Studies from the USA, Europe and Asia all indicate that adolescence is a time of sexual vulnerability" says Dr Hayter. "The UK certainly reflects this trend and has one of the highest rates of teenage pregnancies and STIs in Europe. In some areas it is common to see pregnancy rates of up to 19 per 1000 in the 13–16 age group."

Distinct trends can also be seen from the international literature, including sexual activity at a younger age and increased risk taking, such as unprotected sex with new or casual partners. This behaviour is strongly influenced by social and contextual factors closely related to peer pressure, alcohol use and gender power.

"Nurses working in sexual health clinics used by young people should be aware of the ways in which their clients think about sex and relationships" concludes Dr Hayter.

"Providing information and contraception is only one element of promoting sexual health.

"When it comes to female clients, nurses should develop interventions that can strengthen self-esteem and teach young girls how to respond positively to the social pressures they face around sex.

"It would also be helpful to encourage young male clients to empathise with their female partners.

"Last, but definitely not least, clinics need to treat alcohol use by their clients as a higher priority, integrating advice and help about harmful drinking into their sexual health promotion work."

> "By normalizing and giving permission for sexual activity, permission that seems to override parental disapproval, media may be the most powerful and universal influence on young people's sexual attitudes and decision-making."

Media Influence on Teenage Sexuality Is Significant

Michael Rich

Michael Rich is a pediatrician and director of the Center on Media and Child Health at Children's Hospital in Boston. He is also an associate professor at Harvard Medical School and the Harvard School of Public Health. In the following viewpoint, Rich begins with an overview of how media are used by adolescents and young people, who acknowledge that they depend on the Internet and television to learn about sexuality. According to Rich, several studies have documented the impact of sexual content in the entertainment media on young people. Much of this research reveals that sexual relationships portrayed in the media reinforce gender stereotypes and fail to explore negative conse-

Michael Rich, "Virtual Sexuality: The Influence of Entertainment Media on Sexual Attitudes and Behavior," *Managing the Media Monster: The Influence of Media (From Television to Text Messages) on Teen Sexual Behavior and Attitudes*, Edited by Jane D. Brown, National Campaign to Prevent Teen and Unplanned Pregnancy, 2008, pp. 24–28, 30–32. Copyright © 2008 by The National Campaign to Prevent Teen and Unplanned Pregnancy. All rights reserved. Reproduced by permission.

quences, often promoting unhealthy sexual behavior among teens. Given the strong influence of the Internet, television, and cell phones on today's teenagers, and the easy access to information that these sources provide, Rich suggests that a strong effort is needed to direct the power of the media to educate adolescents and young adults about sexual health.

As you read, consider the following questions:

1. How does having a television in the bedroom impact sexual activity among teens?

2. According to the author, media establishes norms of acceptable sexual behavior for teens. How?

3. What safety measures can help reduce teen exposure to sexual content on the Internet?

Determining young people's actual exposure and response to sexual content in media is the first step to assessing the influence of media on their sexual attitudes and behaviors. Research shows that exposure to sexual material in media starts early. One study found that children ages 6 to 11 are attracted to and watch TV with sexual themes and references, such as dating shows, soap operas, and sitcoms, in part because they are accessing "forbidden fruit" aimed at more mature viewers. In an early study examining how well young people comprehend sexual content on TV, pre-teens and teens were found to have good grasp of sexual innuendo, but those aged 12 understood significantly less than those aged 14 and 16.

One study found that 75 percent of surveyed college students recalled first seeing explicit sexual media content as minors and 15 percent said that they had enduring thoughts about the sexual content. They reported physical responses such as sexual arousal, avoidance, tension, and nausea, and emotional responses, including disgust, shock, embarrassment, and interest in the material.

Seeking Out Media with Sexual Content

Girls in early adolescence have been found to choose media idols consistent with their stage of romantic interest—focusing on feminine idols before they are interested in boys, then transitioning to masculine idols as their sexuality develops. Thus, media may serve as a crucible for developing sexuality. As young people grapple with their own emerging sexual identities, they may seek out models in the media, wrestling with their initial attraction-repulsion to sexual issues, evolving into virtual relationships with celebrities, and finally attraction to others in real life. Adolescents acknowledge that they use media to learn about sexuality, relationships, and love. Youth approach and respond to media from their own life experiences, so ethnicity, gender, class, and developmental stage all influence their media choices. Although some adolescents do not see people or lives such as theirs reflected in the media, when teens *do* see people or images in media to which they relate, they are more likely to be influenced. White and black middle school students have been shown to have distinct and different TV viewing preferences. In a study from 2001, the top 10 shows viewed by African-American adolescents all featured African-American characters and none were regularly viewed by more than 16% of the white adolescents. Among the 140 most popular TV shows, only four were regularly watched by more than one-third of each race/gender group.

Testing the theory that we consume media that reflect and validate our experience, studies have investigated whether preference for media with sexual content varies between sexually active and inactive youth. One analysis of media viewing habits among pregnant and non-pregnant African-American and white adolescent girls ages 13 to 19 found that pregnant girls of both races had significantly greater exposure to sexual content in soap operas, primetime TV, and R-rated films, compared to non-pregnant adolescent girls, although another study found no differences. Adolescent girls who reached physical maturation earlier showed more interest in sexual media, viewed more R-rated movies, accessed more media information on dating, contraception, and sexually transmitted infections (STIs), and were more likely to perceive of media as normalizing or giving societal permission for sexual activity.

Exposure to Sexuality on the Internet

With the rapid rise of Internet use among children and youth, exposure to explicit sexual material and vulnerability to online sexual interactions with others has been of increased concern to parents and to society. Children now start using the Internet quite young and many report problematic experiences. Dutch studies with children ages 8 to 12 found that half had negative experiences on the Internet, with girls reporting being disturbed by online content, especially pornography, more often than boys. As youth get older and more experienced, their Internet use becomes less accessible to parental oversight, but many still feel unsafe. Among 7th–10th graders in the Midwest who reported using a computer 4.8 days a week on average, 25 percent reported feeling unsafe online, more than half of those due to strangers or acquaintances using the Internet to connect with them in a sexual manner. . . .

Adolescents and young adults who use the Internet the most, particularly those who use it to connect with others for romantic or sexual relationships, are at highest risk of being exposed to unwanted material or solicitations. Because the Internet offers a variety of models for connecting with others and provides the "three As"—Accessibility, Affordability, and (perceived) Anonymity—it is attractive (particularly for those who feel isolated or marginalized) as a way to "try out" relationships. Problems have arisen, however, when youth try to transform Internet-established connections into face-to-face relationships. One study supports the premise that youth mainly use the Internet for social purposes, with IM [instant messaging] being the most prevalent activity, but this study found that more than half the young users had misrepresented who they were online, often portraying themselves as older and more sexually experienced than they actually were. The explosive growth of social networking sites has made it common, if not expected, for young people to have a MySpace or Facebook page with which to present themselves to the world. Research on Internet chat rooms, which preceded social networking sites as a virtual venue for meeting and interacting, found that younger adolescents were more likely to provide information about their actual identities, while older teens were more likely to communicate explicitly sexual material. Some studies have shown that developing an Internet-based social network led to an unhealthy retreat from real-life interaction with peers.

Relationships Observed Between Media Exposure and Sexual Attitudes and Behavior

Given the prevalence of sexual content in popular media available to children and adolescents, it is important to test the hypothesis that young people's exposure to sexual media influences their perceptions and expectations of relationships and contributes to the development of their sexual attitudes and behaviors. Media portrayals of sex as a fun, carefree, and common activity that does not warrant concerns, cautions, contraception, or consequences may cultivate similar beliefs and influence sexual behaviors among youth. These studies are designed to assess statistical associations between viewing specific media and viewers' sexual attitudes or behaviors, the odds of exposure and outcomes grouping together; they cannot demonstrate causality (that the exposure causes outcomes). In the few cases where researchers controlled for other factors that may have affected the outcomes of interest, such as family connectedness, media literacy, access to sex education or confidential reproductive healthcare, these controls are explained.

In 1991, although they did not measure media content, [J.L.] Peterson and colleagues found an association between duration of TV viewing and early initiation of sexual intercourse among adolescents. This finding was supported by [J.D.] Brown and [S.F.] Newcomer, who found that junior high school students who watched television with more sexual content were more likely to have initiated sexual activity than those who watched less sexual media content. What remained unclear from these cross-sectional studies was whether youth who watched more sexual media content were more likely to have sex or whether those who were having sex were more likely to watch content that reflected their experience.

A decade later, a longitudinal prospective survey of 1,461 youth ages 12 to 17 who were interviewed three times over three years by [R.L.] Collins and colleagues showed that those with high exposure to sexual content on TV were twice as likely to initiate sexual intercourse in an upcoming year. They also became sexually active, on average, six months earlier than their peers with low exposure to televised sexual content. Girls viewed more sexual content on TV than did boys, and younger adolescents viewed more sexual content than older adolescents. Having a TV in the bedroom and friends who approved of sexual activity predicted higher exposure to sexual content. Building on these findings, a recent analysis using an additional wave of these data found that exposure to high sexual content on TV at baseline is associated with an increased risk of teen pregnancy over the subsequent three years.

Broadening beyond TV, Brown and colleagues conducted a similar longitudinal study assessing the influence of exposure to sexual content in four media (TV, movies, music, and magazines) popular with 1,017 early adolescents (ages 12 to 14). They found that the quintile of teens who consumed the greatest amount of sexual media content in early adolescence were more than twice as likely as those with lighter sexual media diets to have initiated sexual intercourse by the time they were 16 years old.

Music and Television Matter

Music is often the medium that defines and may help shape young people's romantic ideals and expectations. Recent research has associated frequent listening to music that has degrading sexual lyrics with adolescents' higher likelihood of initiating sexual intercourse and with more rapid progress through non-coital sexual activities. Females who listened to heavy metal music have been found more likely to have sex without contraception and male heavy metal fans had more sexual partners and lower respect for women than did fans of other musical genres. When compared to peers, 12- to 14-year-olds exposed to sexual content in popular music were at increased risk for light sexual activity (e.g., kissing, touching), while those exposed to sexual content in movies were at elevated risk for both light and heavy sexual activity (e.g., oral sex, intercourse).

The influence of TV exposure on sexual attitudes, expectations, and behaviors may depend on the sex roles and sexual expectations portrayed. Adolescent girls who watch more prime-time TV, particularly those who identify strongly with the characters, have been shown more likely to view sex as a recreational activity. In another study, which compared amounts of TV watched and program formats, viewing more TV, especially soap operas, was related to younger initiation to dating and having a greater number of dating partners. Those who watched romantic programming were more likely to endorse traditional gender role beliefs than those who viewed other formats. In contrast, viewing non-romantic dramas was correlated with participants having less traditional gender roles and more dating partners. Among college students, watching MTV was the most powerful predictor of females' sexual attitudes and number of sexual partners, but soap opera viewing, self-esteem, and relationship involvement were the best predictors of their male counterparts' number of sexual partners.

Females who had substantial exposure to sexual content on TV have been found to expect sex at a relatively early stage in relationships, but not to have expectations regarding variety of sexual behaviors. On the other hand, men who watch a substantial amount of televised sexual content expect more variety in behaviors, but their expectations about the timing of sexual activity in a relationship are similar to men who watch less sexual content. Exposure to televised sex has been found to predict having sexually active friends, safe-sex self-efficacy, and less romantic, more cynical expectations from sex.

[S.] Jackson and others have expressed specific concern that the media's portrayal of females as passive recipients and males as active instigators of sexual activity may interfere with the successful negotiation of safe sex. One study found that young women who watched more TV, particularly soap operas and prime-time dramas, were less likely to feel in control of and happy with their sexual activity than their peers who watched less TV. Females reported less sense of control over their own sexual encounters after watching TV program episodes of sexual women attracting males and men avoiding commitment in relationships. . . .

The Internet Is Pervasive

For many young users, the Internet is as familiar and comfortable a place in which to meet new people, make friends, and nurture relationships as the local shopping mall. As a result of its ease, ubiquity, and illusion of privacy, the Internet has emerged as a new, but little understood, environment for meeting sexual partners. Ninth graders in Minnesota who used chat rooms to connect with others were more likely than those who did not frequent chat rooms to demonstrate risk behaviors, including substance abuse and sexual intercourse. Outbreaks of STIs [sexually transmitted infections] have been traced to chat rooms specializing in specific sexual interests

"You don't need to tell me about the birds and the bees,"
I downloaded it all from the Internet."

A.BACALL

"You don't need to tell me about the birds and the bees," cartoon by Aaron Bacall, www.CartoonStock.com. Copyright © Aaron Bacall. Reproduction rights obtainable from www.CartoonStock.com.

because they have served the traditional functions of bars, clubs and bathhouses by introducing people of similar sexual persuasions who arrange to meet for high risk anonymous encounters.

After controlling for age, gender, race, and socioeconomic status, a survey of 471 7th and 8th grade girls found that perceived societal permission for sexual activity communicated in popular media was found to be strongly associated with sexual intentions and activity. The amount of media consumption accounted for 13 percent of the variance in intending to have sex in the near future, 10 percent of the variance in light sexual activity, and 8 percent of the variance in heavy sexual activity. A similar analysis showed that media normalization of and permission for sexual activity may be more powerful than parental influence. Data from the National Longitudinal Study of Adolescent Health demonstrated that adolescents whose parents limited their TV viewing to less than two hours a day had about half the rate of sexual initiation as adolescents whose parents strongly disapproved of sex, but did not limit TV viewing, resulting in the adolescent watching more than two hours of TV a day.

Exposure to sexual content in media has consistently been associated with increases in sexual risk behaviors among youth. In longitudinal studies, the exposure to sexual media as a child or early adolescent predicts earlier sexual initiation, more sexual partners, and higher risk of pregnancy or STIs. Media have become a ubiquitous superpeer from which young people learn what to expect and what is expected of them. By normalizing and giving permission for sexual activity, permission that seems to override parental disapproval, media may be the most powerful and universal influence on young people's sexual attitudes and decision-making. . . .

Implications of Media Impact

Children and youth spend more time using media than they do engaged in any other activity. They have more opportunity to learn about themselves, their sexuality, and the nature of relationships from media than they do from school, parents, or any other source, particularly in communities where sex education is limited or prohibited. Sexual content is prevalent and easy to access in a variety of media platforms, from TV to the Internet, even at very young ages. In the Media Age, young people can obtain sexual images, narratives, and information more easily than ever before. Today's children and young people can access more explicit pornography with a single mouse click than most of their parents have seen in their life-times. Driven by the need for novelty to capture a larger audi-ence share, sexual portrayals in media are increasingly fre-quent and explicit—what was shocking and attention-grabbing last week is old news today.

Because children and youth spend so much time with TV, music, and the Internet, media may be the source of first im-pressions and ongoing perceptions that are critical to the de-velopment of a young person's sexual attitudes, expectations, and behaviors. One area of concern yet to be researched is the effect of early, formative exposures to sex occurring in the form of Internet pornography. The Internet is primarily a venue of commerce. Sex is presented as a commodity that can be bought, sold, and traded. If young people's initial explora-tions of sex happen in the context of the sexual marketplace rather than learning about connecting and developing rela-tionships with others, how are they to develop healthy con-cepts of romance, relationships, and responsibilities around sex? Seen in this context, the phenomenon of "friends with benefits," in which young people with no romantic relation-ship have sex with each other out of boredom or a need for "something to do," is hardly surprising.

Beyond providing first exposures to sexual material, for many youth the media establish norms for behavior and tac-itly give permission for sexual activity by implying that "ev-erybody is doing it." Research indicates that exposure to sexual media influences young people to overestimate the prevalence of sexual activity among their peers and to lower their own resistance to initiating sex. Given the limited, but significant evidence linking exposure to sexual content in entertainment media with subsequent changes in sexual attitudes and in-creases in risk behaviors, it is important that parents, health-care providers, and others committed to the healthy develop-ment of children and adolescents understand and respond to entertainment media as a powerful environmental influence on young people's health and well-being.

Rating Systems Need Improvement

Media rating systems have been established by the entertainment industry to indicate the age-appropriateness of media content. Media producers encourage parents to use them, claiming they are accurate and effective, but many parents rightfully distrust the ratings. In a study that asked parents to independently rate the appropriateness of TV programs, movies, and computer/video games for use by children, current industry rating systems were consistently more lenient, varying by as much as 50 percent from what parents thought was right for their children. In part, distrust of the ratings results from the fact that, as currently designed and implemented, entertainment media ratings are focused on social values rather than objective health outcomes. As a result, ratings are inconsistent, shifting in the winds of changing social norms. If parents do not share the values of the ratings board, they feel, rightly, that the ratings do not measure what they feel to be important. Another problem posed by the values-based ratings is the observed "backlash effect" of youth seeking material with more mature ratings to taste "the forbidden fruit" and establish themselves as individuals able to make choices independent from what their parents want for them.

Internet safety measures have included technological fixes, such as software to filter or block the Internet from those it might threaten . . . , although there is legitimate concern that such software may hinder use of the Internet by youth to search for critical health information. Increased supervision by adults and restrictions on media access result in reduced exposure, both in duration and content. Both filtering software and education on Internet safety were found to reduce youth exposure to pornography. Monitoring a chat room has been shown to effectively decrease the amount of profanity, but did not affect the prevalence of sexual language and conversation.

Comprehensive assessments of the research findings have come to the conclusion that rating systems, legal or industry restrictions, and technological "fixes" cannot be totally effective in protecting youth from the deleterious effects of media. Building on the research, key recommendations from the American Academy of Pediatrics and the American Psychological Association are for adults to help children and adolescents limit their exposure to sexual content in media, to teach them to deconstruct and decipher the messages they receive from media and popular culture, and for media producers to balance media portrayals of sex with accurate and practical information about the potential consequences of sexual activity.

Education and Information Are Crucial

Young viewers and their families need to be educated about how to use media wisely and safely. When asked directly about the relationship between sex in media and sexual behavior, nearly two-thirds (65 percent) of both adolescent and adult viewers denied any relationship, but 45 percent believed that sexual content in media could help start good conversations between youth and adults, with 19 percent believing that children could learn something good from this exposure. In practice, family discussions about media content and regulation of media consumption are often used as a way for parents to communicate moral values to their pre-teen children. As a public health intervention, themes communicated through broadcast television programming are much more effective when parents have watched the program with the young person and discussed it, as demonstrated by a single episode of *Friends* that portrayed condom failure resulting in pregnancy. Nearly one-third of the viewers surveyed (1.67 million 12- to 17-year-old viewers saw the episode) were able to recall the information that condoms were between 95 percent and 100 percent effective. Almost half of the adolescents that watched and discussed the episode with an adult recalled the condom efficacy information, which was nearly twice the proportion of those who did not discuss the episode with an adult. Condom advertisements on TV were approved of by 83 percent of parents, 89 percent of female adolescents, and 92 percent of male adolescents. Although parents' perceptions of their 11- to 16-year-old children's Internet exposure to negative sexual content were significantly lower than children's actual exposure, children whose parents reported high family cohesion and shared Internet activities were significantly less likely to be exposed to negative Internet content than those with lower family cohesion and fewer shared Internet experiences.

Media use policies in the home can positively affect viewing habits. Families that are connected, communicative, and aware can be the most protective factor in a child's life. However, as children progress into and through adolescence, the authority of parents and other adult figures diminishes, so the best protections are those that we can instill in youth themselves. Education has been proposed and implemented as a key part of health intervention. As has been demonstrated with smoking portrayals, "pre-inoculating" viewers with an educational "reality check" immediately before the risky media exposure is perhaps the most effective educational intervention. Media literacy, the discipline of critical viewing of media and reducing unhealthy media exposure, is starting to show promise as an intervention on other media-related health effects, such as obesity and aggression. There is every reason to believe that increasing young people's media literacy would be a successful strategy to counter the influence of media on sexual attitudes and behaviors as well.

Media Can Be Used as an Ally

Media have our young people's time and attention. Ultimately, . . . the most effective response to media influence will be to use media to educate about sexual health. TV has been shown to be a powerful tool for changing hearts and minds about rape, homosexuality, and open communication about safe sex practices. Popular music can be used to explore sexual topics and promote health, as has been done in such curricula as "Exploring your Sexuality Through Current Rock."

Today, we have more capability to connect, communicate, and entertain ourselves than ever before in history. Although their current quantity and quality of media exposure places adolescents at increased risk, it is a risk that, with increased awareness, education, and empowerment, they can manage. Media and the popular culture they create are so ubiquitous and insistent that many parents and caregivers often feel overwhelmed; it can be tempting to give up. However, the youth know, and we must all remember, that media are tools that we can use instead of letting them use us. New media technology and applications, from video-capable cell phones to Web 2.0 sites that promote creation and distribution of original media created by youth, present real opportunities for taking back the media and bringing forth the voice of the youth we serve. Through using media to connect, communicate, and build community, young people can simultaneously learn to assess the real from the false and, instead of allowing media to control them, control the media to share the knowledge, experience, and strategies that will allow them to grow up to be healthy, responsible, and safe.

| "We found no accelerating or hastening effect of exposure to sexy media content on sexual debut."

Media Influence on Teenage Sexuality Is Exaggerated

Laurence Steinberg and Kathryn C. Monahan

Laurence Steinberg is a professor in the Department of Psychology at Temple University. Kathryn C. Monahan is affiliated with the Social Development Research Group in the School of Social Work at the University of Washington. In the following viewpoint, the authors report on a study they conducted about the impact of media with sexual content on adolescent sexual behavior. Two recent studies linking early sexual activity among teens as a result of exposure to sexual content in the media have caused alarm among parents and medical professionals. Steinberg and Monahan claim that the results of these surveys may be flawed because of their assumption that media exposure causes early sexual activity. Instead, the authors suggest, a link between certain types of media and sexual activity may be the result of a propensity among some youth to seek out sexual media content. To support their hypothesis, Steinberg and Monahan use data

Laurence Steinberg and Kathryn C. Monahan, "Adolescents' Exposure to Sexy Media Does Not Hasten the Initiation of Sexual Intercourse," *Developmental Psychology*, August 2, 2010, pp. 1–2, 9–14. Copyright © 2010 by American Psychological Association. All rights reserved. Reproduced by permission.

*from the same studies to show that there is no evidence linking
initiation of sexual intercourse with exposure to sexual images in
media.*

As you read, consider the following questions:

1. According to the authors, which medium provides the
   most explicit and frequent sexual imagery to teens?

2. In the authors' view, for what reasons are adult concerns
   about the adverse impact of adolescents' exposure to
   sexual content in the media understandable?

3. List three well-established risk factors for early sexual
   activity.

American adolescents are bombarded with sexual imagery
in television programs, films, music videos and on the Internet. According to recent analyses, some form of sexual content (including talking about sex, passionate kissing, intimate touching, and explicit sexual intercourse) appears in 70% of all television programs, with sexual talk appearing in 68% of shows (at a rate exceeding four scenes per hour) and sexual behavior in 35% of shows (at a rate of two scenes per hour). Implied sexual intercourse is portrayed in 11% of all television shows. The presence of sexual content is even higher in prime-time shows (six scenes per hour) and higher still in the shows most watched by teenagers (nearly seven scenes per hour). Sexual content on television is thought to have increased substantially over the past decade. Although comparably large-scale systematic analyses of sexual content in media other than television have not been conducted (in part because the sheer number of songs, films, and Internet sites available at any point in time is so large), smaller scale studies of these other media indicate that adolescents' exposure to sexual imagery is even more common in music lyrics than in television programs, and comparable in film and television.

Concerns About the Impact of Media on Adolescent Sexual Health

The high frequency with which entertainment media contain sexual content is of particular interest to those interested in the health of adolescents, for at least two reasons. First, adolescents are voracious consumers of mass media, with the average teenager exposed to mass media for 6 hours each day; when multitasking is taken into account, this figure increases to 8 hours. Among early adolescents (11–14 years), television accounts for about 40% of this exposure, and film and other prerecorded videos (some of which are prerecorded television programs) account for another 10% or so; among older teenagers (15–18 years), the two media account for about 40% combined.

Second, a good deal of adolescents' sexual behavior puts their health at risk. A substantial portion of adolescents fail to use condoms, exposing themselves to the risks of pregnancy and sexually transmitted infections (STIs). This problem is especially severe among younger teenagers, who, if sexually active, are less likely to practice safe sex than their older counterparts. Despite considerable efforts to educate American teenagers about the dangers of unsafe sex, the United States still has one of the highest rates of teen pregnancy in the world, and in recent years, the rate of teen childbearing in the United States has risen. The United States also has one of the highest rates of STIs in the world, with adolescents comprising one of the highest risk groups. One analysis estimates that the treatment of new cases of STIs among young adolescents costs American taxpayers $6.5 billion annually.

Assumptions That Exposure to Mass Media Affects Sexual Activity

It is widely assumed that adolescents' exposure to sexual content in the mass media influences their sexual activity and may contribute to sexual risk taking. Portrayals of sexual activity in mass media favored by teenagers often show the emotional and social consequences of sexual activity (e.g., guilt, disappointment), but less frequently show adverse physical consequences (e.g., pregnancy, STIs). In light of this, and in view of the amount of mass media teenagers are exposed to and the proportion of that exposure that contains sexual content, it is reasonable to think that risky sexual behavior (early sex, unprotected sex, or promiscuous sex) results in part from the impact of mass media on adolescents' attitudes, beliefs, and behavior.

Many studies have documented a correlation between exposure to sexy media and sexual behavior. These studies, however, are limited in the sorts of causal inferences one can draw from them, because it is eminently plausible that interest in sex leads to exposure to sexy media (referred to as *differential selection*), rather than the reverse (referred to as *socialization*). To address these inferential limitations, several recent studies have examined this issue with longitudinal data, studying the over-time impact of media exposure on sexual activity after taking into account characteristics of adolescents that may predispose them to sexy media exposure (e.g., demographic factors, motives to have sex). Two widely cited studies of this type are those of [R.L.] Collins et al. (2004), which examined the effects of exposure to televised sexual content, and [J.] Brown et al. (2006), which examined the effects of exposure to sexual content in the adolescent's entire media diet (television, music, movies, and magazines). Both studies reported that exposure to sexy media content increases the likelihood of sexual activity and, importantly, hastens the initiation of sexual intercourse. . . .

Many Studies Inaccurately Find a Causal Connection

Adults' concern about the potential adverse impact of adolescents' exposure to sexual content on television, in mov-

Media Are Not to Blame

Adolescents who consume the highest amounts of sexy media are already interested in sex.

"A small portion of adolescents are *not* interested in sex. Hormones are part of us," Dr. Lisa Rhodes, an American studies professor, said. "It is like showing someone a picture of food and saying that it will make them eat more. That assumes that the person didn't eat in the first place."

Samantha Krotzer, "Sex, with or Without the TV,"
The Temple News, *September 20, 2010.*

ies, in magazines, and in music lyrics is understandable, given the amount of sexual content these mass media present, the amount of time teenagers spend exposed to them, and the continuing high rates of unwanted pregnancy and STIs among American youth. Many scientists, professionals, and health care practitioners have alerted parents to the potential dangers of exposure to sexy media and have called on the entertainment industry to change its behavior, citing studies that show a significant relationship between sexy media exposure and adolescents' sexual behavior (e.g., American Academy of Pediatrics, 2006). These studies, in turn, draw considerable media attention and generate substantial public interest. According to the website of the American Academy of Pediatrics, "the recognized leader among medical organizations on the issue of media effects on health" ([M.] Rich, 2005), the Collins et al. (2004) study of sexy media exposure and adolescent sexual activity was one of the 10 most frequently read articles in *Pediatrics*, the association's journal, 5 years after the article's initial publication (American Academy of Pediatrics, 2009).

The authors of these studies make strong assertions that imply a causal relationship, as was the case in the specific study whose data are reanalyzed in this report. Although Brown et al. (2006) were admirably cautious in the concluding paragraphs of their article (e.g., "All of the possible alternative explanations for early sexual behavior were not included in this analysis"), the title of their article ("Sexy Media Matter: Exposure to Sexual Content in Music, Movies, Television, and Magazines Predicts Black and White Adolescents' Sexual Behavior") implies a causal link between media exposure and sexual activity (i.e., that the former predicts the latter) as does the article's abstract: "Exposure to sexual content in music, movies, television, and magazines *accelerates* [emphasis added] white adolescents' sexual activity and increases their risk of engaging in early sexual intercourse." Collins et al. (2004), who used a statistical approach that is similar to that employed by Brown et al. and is characterized by the same limitations on the drawing of causal conclusions (but who declined to make their data available for reanalysis), nevertheless write in their abstract that "watching sex on TV predicts and may *hasten* [emphasis added] adolescent sexual initiation" and go so far as to suggest ways that parents might *"reduce the effects* [emphasis added] of sexual content" on their adolescent children.

Analysis Finds No Causal Relationship

The present analysis suggests that parents may have less to worry about than these studies suggest. In our reanalysis of the data used by Brown et al. (2006), we found that using a more stringent approach to accounting for differential selection undoes any apparent effect of sexy media exposure on adolescents' initiation of sexual intercourse. That is, we found no accelerating or hastening effect of exposure to sexy media content on sexual debut once steps were taken to ensure that adolescents with and without high media exposure were matched on their propensity to be exposed to media with sexual content. We note, however, that our analysis focused only on the impact of sexy media exposure on the initiation of intercourse and not on the impact of media exposure on already sexually active teenagers, a question we could not address because the study included too few adolescents who were non-virgins at baseline. We share with many health care practitioners and health educators their concerns over the high rate of unsafe sex among American adolescents. Whether exposure to sexy media impacts condom use or other safe-sex practices among sexually active adolescents remains a question for future research.

Although one can never formally accept the null hypothesis—here, proving that sexy media exposure has no impact—our analysis of the same data set used by Brown et al. (2006) gives us added confidence that our failure to replicate their findings is not due to a lack of statistical power or to the use of different measures. And although we dropped a small number of subjects from our analyses who were included in the original analyses (and whom we dropped because they were already sexually experienced at baseline), our failure to replicate the Brown et al. findings is not due to this, because we were able to replicate their earlier findings with this slightly reduced sample. Rather, the difference between the findings is entirely attributable to our employing a more stringent method to control for differences between adolescents who do and do not expose themselves to sexy media content. Whether comparable reanalyses of data from other studies, employing different measures and samples but more conservative controls for differential selection, would yield similar conclusions awaits further study and the willingness of other researchers to make their data available for secondary analysis.

Most developmental scientists agree that it is important to distinguish between sexual activity that is initiated prior to age 16, which does not have negative correlates, and sexual activity that begins later in development. Because precocious sexual activity may be associated with problematic functioning, and because younger adolescents are less likely to practice safe sex than their older peers, it is important to understand the factors that predict early sexual activity. Some factors, such as parental permissiveness, parent-adolescent conflict, and having sexually active friends are well-established risk factors for early sexual debut. Others, such as exposure to sexy media, are factors often believed to influence adolescents to start having sex but that, on closer inspection, may not actually have this effect. It is easy to point our collective finger at the entertainment industry, but it is likely that the most important influences on adolescents' sexual behavior may be closer to home than to Hollywood.

Periodical and Internet Sources Bibliography

The following articles have been selected to supplement the diverse views presented in this chapter.

Bill Albert	"Parental Influence and Teen Pregnancy," March 1, 2007. www.education.com.
Barna Group	"Teen Role Models: Who They Are, Why They Matter," 2011. www.barna.org.
Kia Bryan	"Sexy Media Does Not Lead to Teenage Sex," FYI Living, October 7, 2010. www.fyiliving .com.
Steve Doughty	"Computers and TV Blamed for Teenage Violence and Casual Sex," *Daily Mail*, February 3, 2009. www.dailymail.co.uk.
Roger Friedland	"Guilty Pleasures: Religion and Sex Among American University Students," *The Huffington Post*, July 20, 2010. www.huffingtonpost.com.
Amanda Gardner	"U.S. Pediatricians Decry Media's Portrayal of Sex," *Consumer Health News*, August 31, 2010.
Norman Horowitz	"Time to Differentiate Harmful from Harmless," *Television Week*, June 4, 2007.
Olivia Lichtenstein	"How the Faceless and Amoral World of Cyberspace Has Created a Deeply Disturbing . . . Generation SEX," *Daily Mail*, January 28, 2009. www.dailymail.co.uk.
Robin Summerfield	"Sex Sells . . . Even to Children," *Edmonton Journal* (Alberta), September 19, 2008.
Jennie Yabroff	"The Myths of Teen Sex," *Newsweek*, June 9, 2008.

What Are Some
Significant Teen
Sexuality Issues?

Chapter Preface

A 2010 study conducted by the Case Western Reserve University School of Medicine concluded that teens who hypertext (send more than 120 text messages a day) are three times more likely to have sex and use alcohol and drugs versus teens who don't send as many text messages. Although texting was not identified as the cause of early sexual activity among teens, the study drew a strong link between excessive texting and risky sexual behavior. The Case Western study was the first of its kind, and it confirmed a notion held by many parents and educators who worry about the impact of texting on teenage behavior in general, and sexual activity in particular.

The findings of the Case Western study are supported by the results of an online survey commissioned by CosmoGirl .com and The National Campaign to Prevent Teen and Unplanned Pregnancy. The survey revealed that 20 percent of teens (13–19) have used their phones to send sexually explicit messages, while 39 percent of the 1,280 respondents reported that sexually suggestive messages are the most commonly exchanged subject matter in phone texts. A smaller number of survey respondents admitted to exchanging sexually suggestive images. Among those who noted that they send or post sexually suggestive messages via their cell phone, "hooking up" with another person or getting to know someone were cited as their main reasons for doing so. The teens admitted that they were aware that "sending/posting sexually suggestive content has an impact on their behavior," but they view sending and posting sexually explicit messages as a "fun and flirtatious" activity. Although exchanging sexual banter is common and normal during teen years, the impact of texting a message versus the face-to-face conversations of the past is very different. Many teens admit that they would likely be uncomfortable saying things in person that they are willing to text to another person, especially when it comes to sexual activities.

Teens use cell phones and text messages as their primary means of communication. In 2008, according to an Associated Press survey, one out of every four teens had a cell phone, and a large percentage of them were sending or receiving approximately 3,000 text messages each month. Given the connection between texting and sexual activity documented by Case Western, parents of teens may feel they have cause for concern. In the case of teens from lower-income families, one-parent households, and households in which the parents are working, the risk factors are even higher. Further complicating the issue for teens who text sexually explicit material is the fact that such behavior can be illegal. Many teens do not comprehend the emotional and legal impact of these activities and are unaware that under current law, the exchange of any sexual content related to a minor is a prosecutable offense, even if the information was exchanged consensually.

Navigating technological advances and their impact is only one of the challenges facing today's teens. In the viewpoints in the following chapter, commentators discuss other significant teen sexuality issues.

> "Simply put, if more children in this country were born to parents who are ready and able to take care of them, we would see a significant reduction in a host of social problems afflicting children in the United States."

Teen Pregnancy Is a Significant Problem

The National Campaign to Prevent Teen and Unplanned Pregnancy

The National Campaign to Prevent Teen and Unplanned Pregnancy seeks to decrease teen pregnancy. The National Campaign conducts research, publishes informational articles, and supports legislation that advances its mission. The following viewpoint reveals that the United States continues to have one of the highest rates of teen pregnancy among developed nations, resulting in many negative outcomes for children born to teen parents. In addition to the personal cost borne by the children of teen parents, teen pregnancy and its related costs place a significant burden on federal, state, and local taxpayers.

National Campaign to Prevent Teen and Unplanned Pregnancy, "Why It Matters: Linking Teenage Pregnancy Prevention to Other Critical Issues," March 2010. www.the nationalcampaign.org. Copyright © 2010 by The National Campaign to Prevent Teen and Unplanned Pregnancy. All rights reserved. Reproduced by permission.

As you read, consider the following questions:

1. What percentage of young girls become pregnant in the United States before they reach the age of twenty? List three critical social issues linked to early pregnancy and childbearing.

2. What is the estimated cost of teen childbearing to US taxpayers?

3. List two significant health problems afflicting babies born to teen mothers.

Despite a one-third decline since the early 1990s, the United States still has the highest rates of teen pregnancy and birth among comparable countries. In fact, 3 in 10 girls in this country become pregnant by age 20—over 750,000 teen pregnancies annually.

Early pregnancy and childbearing are closely linked to a host of other critical social issues, including poverty and income disparity, overall child well-being, out-of-wedlock births, and education, to name just a few. Simply put, if more children in this country were born to parents who are ready and able to care for them, we would see a significant reduction in a host of social problems afflicting children in the United States, from school failure and crime to child abuse and neglect.

The Effects of Teen Pregnancy on Society

What if? The teen birth rate declined by one-third between 1991 and 2002. What if it had not? What if the teen birth rate in the United States had stayed at the 1991 level?

- 1.2 million more children would have been born to teen mothers.

- 460,000 additional children would be living in poverty.

- 700,000 more children would be living in single-mother households.

An Increase in US Pregnancy and Birth Rates Among Young Women

By 1990 or 1991, the pregnancy rate among teenagers and young women had begun a steady and consistent decline. A decrease in both birth *and* abortion rates among these women signaled that both intended and unintended pregnancy rates were declining among these age-groups. Recent research concluded that almost all of the decline in the pregnancy rate between 1995 and 2002 among 18–19-year-olds was attributable to increased contraceptive use. Among women aged 15–17, about one-quarter of the decline during the same period was attributable to reduced sexual activity and three-quarters to increased contraceptive use.

But, for the first time since the early 1990s, overall rates of pregnancy and birth—and, to a lesser extent, rates of abortion—among teenagers and young women increased from 2005 to 2006. It is too soon to tell whether this reversal is simply a short-term fluctuation, a more lasting stabilization or the beginning of a longer-term increase. Preliminary data on births for 2007 show a further increase in the birthrate among all women, including teenagers and those aged 20–24.

US Teenage Pregnancies, Births and Abortions:
National and State Trends and Trends by Race and Ethnicity,
Guttmacher Institute, 2010.

The decrease in the teen birth rate between 1995 and 2002 is directly responsible for:

- 26% of the decrease in the number of children under age six living in poverty.

- 68% of the decrease in the number of children under age six living with single mothers.

What are the chances? What are the chances of a child growing up in poverty if: (1) the mother gave birth as a teen, (2) the parents were unmarried when the child was born, and (3) the mother did not receive a high school diploma or GED.

- 27% if one of these things happens.

- 42% if two of these things happen.

- 64% if three of these things happen.

- But, if *none* of these things happen, a child's chance of growing up in poverty is 7%.

Put another way, if these three things happen, a child's chance of growing up in poverty is *nine times greater* than if none of these things happen.

Public Costs. Teen childbearing is costly to the public sector—federal, state, and local governments and the taxpayers who support them.

- Teen childbearing costs taxpayers at least $9 billion each year, including public sector health care costs, increased child welfare costs, increased prison costs, and lost tax revenue.

- Put another way, between 1991 and 2004 there were over 6 million births to teens in the United States. The estimate cumulative public costs of teen childbearing during this time period is $161 billion.

- Due to the dramatic decline in the teen birth rate between 1991 and 2004, taxpayers saved an estimated $6.7 billion in 2004 alone.

Poverty and Income Disparity. Continuing to reduce teen pregnancy will help sustain recent decreases in poverty.

- Two-thirds of families begun by a young unmarried mother are poor.

- Approximately one-quarter of teen mothers go on welfare within 3 years of the child's birth.

Overall Child Well-Being. The children of teen mothers bear the greatest burden of teen pregnancy and childbearing and are at increased risk for a number of economic, social, and health problems.

- The children of teen mothers are more likely to be born prematurely and at low birthweight and are two times more likely to suffer abuse and neglect compared to children of older mothers.

- The daughters of teen mothers are three times more likely to become teen mothers themselves when compared to the daughters of mothers who were age 20–21.

Out-of-Wedlock Births and Marriage. Reducing teen pregnancy will decrease out-of-wedlock births and increase the proportion of children born to married couples.

- About half of all non-marital first births occur to teens.

- Teens who have a non-marital birth are significantly less likely to be married by age 35 than those who do not have babies as teens.

Child Welfare. Teens in foster care are more likely to get pregnant than teens not in the foster care system, and children born to adolescent parents are more likely than children born to older mothers to enter the foster care system.

- Teen girls in foster care are two and a half times more likely than their peers not in foster care to experience a pregnancy by age 19.

- Children born to teen parents are more likely than those born to older parents to end up in foster care or have multiple caretakers throughout their childhood.

> *"Teenage parenting does not particularly cause poor outcomes for mothers and their children."*

Teen Pregnancy Is Not a Significant Problem

Amelia Gentleman

Amelia Gentleman writes for the Guardian. *She has won several awards for her work, including an Amnesty International Hong Kong Human Rights Press Award in 2007. In the following viewpoint, Gentleman discusses research that contradicts traditionally held beliefs that teen pregnancy is a symbol of a broken social structure. A new study discloses that teenage pregnancy can challenge young parents to higher levels of achievement and motivation. According to the author, instead of castigating teen parents, politicians should focus on helping solve the social and economic issues that precede a teenager's decision to have a baby. The reality is that many teen mothers have positive attitudes about their pregnancies, and many use the opportunity to become more connected and responsible members of society.*

As you read, consider the following questions:

1. According to the editors of the study cited in the viewpoint, what are some of the stereotypes linked to teenage mothers?

2. What are some of the reasons why politicians strive to tackle perceived problems related to teenage pregnancy?

3. Instead of preventing teenage pregnancy, what policy improvements does the author cite as necessary to improve living conditions for young parents?

Teenage pregnancy is not the symbol of a broken society, as claimed by many politicians, but can be a positive force for good, a study published next week [February 2010] will say.

The research describes how teenage parenthood has been linked by politicians and the media with "moral and cultural breakdown", but says it should be seen as "more opportunity than catastrophe".

The study, *Teenage Parenthood: What's the Problem?*, challenges preconceptions, arguing that many teenage mothers are motivated to turn their lives around to provide for their children.

Teen Pregnancy Is Stereotyped

Dr. Claire Alexander, a lecturer at the London School of Economics, and one of the editors of the study, said: "Stereotypes of such young women as poor and ignorant, dysfunctional and immoral, engaging in casual sex and churning out babies who they cannot care for adequately and do not care about in order to gain access to welfare benefits and council housing, often underlie concerns about teenage pregnancy and parenting. However, these stereotypes are not borne out by the research evidence—in fact, quite the contrary."

Politicians, the study says, have focused on attacking teenage pregnancy, rather than tackling the social and economic disadvantage that often prefigures it.

Tony Blair [former British prime minister] described the high teenage birthrate as Britain's "shameful record", and in 1999 the government pledged to halve pregnancies for under-18s by mid-2010, launching the teenage pregnancy strategy to address what it perceived as a critical social and economic problem.

Although the 50% goal is far from being met, Alexander points out that there has been a big decline over the past few decades, and in 2007 only 11.4% of conceptions were to women under 20. "Overall, teenage birthrates are now at around the same level as in the 1950s, that supposed 'golden age' of family," she said.

The study questions the notion that all teenage pregnancies are unplanned and cites evidence suggesting that many teenage parents are "positively ambivalent" towards childbirth. It says: "They do not actually plan it, but would quite like a baby and do not use contraception for that reason."

It concludes that "teenage childbirth does not often result from ignorance or low expectations, it is rarely a catastrophe for young women, and . . . teenage parenting does not particularly cause poor outcomes for mothers and their children".

Pregnancy Can Help Teen Parents

"Our research makes it clear that young parenthood can make sense and be valued and can even provide an impetus for teenage mothers and fathers to strive to provide a better life for their children," Alexander said.

Politicians are at pains to tackle teenage pregnancy because evidence, such as that provided by UNICEF [United Nations International Children's Emergency Fund], suggests that teenage mothers will be much more likely to drop out of school, have low or no qualifications, be unemployed or badly

Teen Pregnancy Is an Opportunity

Teenage birth rates are much lower than in the 1960s and 1970s, and overall are continuing to decline, while few teenage mothers are under sixteen. Age at which pregnancy occurs seems to have little effect on future social outcomes (like employment and income in later life), or on current levels of disadvantage for either parents or their children. Many young mothers and fathers themselves express positive attitudes to parenthood, and mothers usually describe how motherhood makes them feel stronger, more competent, more connected, and more responsible. Many fathers seek to remain connected to their children and provide for their new family. For many young mothers and fathers, parenting seems to provide the impetus to change direction, or build on existing resources, so as to take up education, training and employment. Teenage parenting may be more of an opportunity than a catastrophe.

Simon Duncan, Rosalind Edwards, and Claire Alexander, eds.,
Teenage Parenthood: What's the Problem?,
London, England: Tufnell Press, 2010.

paid, become a victim of neglect or abuse, and become involved in drugs, crime and alcohol.

But the study argues that governments should focus on tackling the original disadvantage often experienced by teenage parents, rather than on attacking their decision to become parents. Its research confirms that children born to teenage mothers are born into disadvantage, but suggests that this disadvantage predates the pregnancy and is not the result of it.

The research also found that many teenage mothers express positive attitudes to motherhood, describing how "motherhood has made them feel stronger, more competent, more connected to family and society and more responsible".

It questions why there is "such a yawning gulf between policy assumptions and the experiences of its subjects" and recommends that policy be focused on improving deprived neighbourhoods and reviving labour markets, rather than on preventing teenage pregnancy.

Teen Parents Face Stigma

"Teenage childbearing in itself can be seen as only a minor social problem. It is not the teenage bit which is particularly important . . . rather it is social and economic disadvantage, which produce poor outcomes," the study argues.

Alexander said: "The [study] explores how this fear of teenage pregnancy is bound up in stereotypes of working-class young women whose out-of-control sexuality has historically concerned the ruling classes as having a dangerous potential for social and moral disorder."

Fiona Weir, chief executive of Gingerbread, the lone parent support group, said: "Single parents of all ages face prejudice and stigma, but this is particularly the case for teenage mothers. This book is a welcome call to look at the real evidence about what works for parents and children, rather than at the stereotypes."

A spokesman for the Department for Children, Schools and Families [in Great Britain] said there had been a reduction of more than 23% in births for under-18s since 1998, to the lowest level for 15 years, and the government was committed to doing more to tackle the issue.

"While many teenage parents manage very well, they and their children are more likely to suffer health, emotional and economic problems. As the vast majority of teenage pregnancies are unplanned, our strategy focuses on giving young people the knowledge, skills and confidence to make positive and informed choices about sexual activity and parenthood," he said.

> "More than 20 percent of all adolescents report having experienced either psychological or physical violence from an intimate partner—and underreporting remains a concern."

Teen Dating Violence Is a Significant Problem

Smita Varia

Smita Varia holds a master's degree and writes for Advocates for Youth, a website providing information on issues related to young people, including sexual health. In the following viewpoint, Varia states that dating violence is a significant problem among adolescents and includes both physical and emotional abuse. More than 20 percent of all adolescents report having experienced some level of trauma related to dating, and the phenomenon affects both males and females. Young people involved in an abusive relationship have a much higher chance of other health problems, and adolescents involved in abusive relationships are less likely than older people to report dating violence because of fear and misguided loyalty. Prevention programs must step up efforts to reach victims of violence, and medical professionals need to make sure that they routinely monitor for signs of abuse among adolescent patients.

As you read, consider the following questions:

1. According to the author, what are some of the most significant negative sexual health outcomes of dating violence?

2. What does the author describe as some of the characteristics of psychological violence among teen couples?

3. What are a few reasons why some teens remain in abusive relationships, in the author's view?

More than 20 percent of all adolescents report having experienced either psychological or physical violence from an intimate partner—and underreporting remains a concern. Dating violence includes psychological or emotional violence, such as controlling behaviors or jealousy; physical violence, such as hitting or punching; and sexual violence such as nonconsensual sexual activity and rape. Female or male teenagers may be the victims and/or perpetrators of dating violence. While both females and males may suffer dating violence, female teens in heterosexual relationships are more likely to be injured, more likely to be sexually assaulted, and more likely to suffer emotionally than are their heterosexual male peers. While little research exists on dating violence among gay, lesbian, bisexual, and transgender (GLBT) youth, research on same-gender violence among GLBT adults shows violence patterns similar to those among heterosexual youth.

Dating violence and abuse can lead to negative sexual health outcomes: the rates of sexually transmitted infections (STIs) and pregnancy are higher for young people who have a history of abuse. Those who have experienced dating violence are also more likely to suffer from mental illness and suicidal thoughts and to be involved in binge drinking, smoking, and/ or fighting.

Programs to prevent dating violence can positively change attitudes if they are appropriately implemented and reach all youth, including those most in need. Health care professionals should routinely screen young people for dating violence.

Dating Violence Includes Psychological, Physical, and Sexual Abuse

- In a national survey, 21 percent of male adolescents and 22 percent of female adolescents reported physical or psychological abuse by an intimate partner. In another national study, 32 percent of adolescents reported experiencing either psychological or physical violence, with the figures being almost identical for both males and females. Both of these studies, along with information from the Centers for Disease Control (CDC), suggest that rates of dating violence are similar across genders.

- In a study conducted at a North Carolina university, 66.7 percent of the respondents reported sexual or physical violence with a partner while in high school.

- According to the CDC, one in 11 adolescents reports physical violence and one in 5 adolescents reports emotional abuse.

- Psychological violence includes uneven power dynamics, control, jealousy and threats regarding the relationship. In one study, 21 percent of teens said that they had been in a relationship with someone who wanted to keep them from seeing friends and family. The same study found that 64 percent of those surveyed had a partner who acted jealous and demanded to know their whereabouts at all times.

- According to data from the 2003 Youth Risk Behavior Surveillance (YRBS), one in eight females and one in

16 males reported being physically forced to have sexual intercourse in their lifetime; nine percent of all adolescents reported having been raped.

- In a study on rape victimization, 22 percent of the women and 3.5 percent of the men surveyed between the ages of 18–29 said that they had been raped during their lifetime. Of these people, more than half of the women and almost three-quarters of the men had been raped before they turned 18 years old.

- According to another national study, 29 percent of the young women surveyed who had ever been in a relationship said they had been pressured to have sex or to engage in sexual activity they did not want.

- In a study of urban youth, 30 percent of the young women reported unwanted sexual experiences in the past twelve months; 13 percent of those incidents were rape or attempted rape.

- Dating violence can lead to a number of problems. One study found that females in violent relationships suffered from post-traumatic stress and dissociation, and males suffered from anxiety, depression and post-traumatic stress. Analysis of the 2001 YRBS found that fighting, binge drinking, smoking, suicidal thoughts and multiple sex partners were linked with a higher prevalence of forced sexual intercourse.

- Young people who have experienced dating violence have been found to carry abusive patterns into future relationships.

Dating Violence in Same-Sex Relationships

Most research conducted on adolescent dating violence has focused on opposite-sex partners. However, two studies on

Dimensions of the Dating Violence Problem

- Almost 30 percent of teens ages 13 to 17 report that they or someone they know has experienced dating violence. Approximately 1 in 5 female high school students reports being abused by a boyfriend.

- Thirty-three percent of teenage girls report having experienced physical violence at the hands of a dating partner. Thirty-eight percent of date rape victims are between 14 and 17 years old. Between 1993 and 1999, 22 percent of all homicides against females ages 16 to 19 were committed by an intimate partner.

- The potential for violent behavior appears to escalate as a dating relationship becomes more serious.

Elizabeth Joyce,
"Teen Dating Violence: Facing the Epidemic,"
National Center for Victims of Crime, 2004.

same-sex partner abuse have found that abuse happens at the same rates of opposite-sex partner violence.

- In a national sample of 117 adolescents, who were selected from the National Longitudinal Study of Adolescent Health because they reported exclusively same-sex intimate relationships, 14.6 percent of males and 26 percent of females reported psychological violence, and 24 percent of males and 28 percent of females reported physical violence.

- Another study that included 184 self-identified GLBT youth measured five types of violence: controlling behaviors, threats to physical safety, emotional abuse, physical abuse, and sexual abuse. Of the males, 43.6 percent had experienced at least one type of abuse from a same-sex partner, and 39.8 percent of the females reported experiencing at least one type of abuse from a same-sex partner. Controlling behaviors were the most common type of abuse, followed by emotional abuse.

- Those in same-sex relationships typically experience the same types of violence as those in opposite-sex relationships, but same-sex partners may have the additional threat and fear of being outed by their partner.

Correlation Between Dating Violence and Sexual Risk

Young women who are in an abusive relationship may be at a higher risk of contracting sexually transmitted infections, including HIV [human immunodeficiency virus], or of becoming pregnant, because the power dynamics within the relationship do not allow them to negotiate condom use. They may fear heightened violence or forced sexual intercourse if they address issues of safer sex. Depression and feelings of sadness or hopelessness in an abusive relationship can also cause risky sexual behavior—the depression may lower the victim's inclination to use protection during intercourse or make them become less concerned about the potential consequences of unprotected sex.

- An analysis of the 2001 YRBS data showed that young women who have experienced dating violence were found to be less likely to use condoms consistently and to be more likely to fear the perceived consequences of negotiating condom use than other young women.

- Analysis of the 2001 YRBS data also showed that rates of recent condom use were significantly lower among young women who had experienced dating violence in the previous year.

- In the same study, young women who reported being hurt in the previous year from dating violence were also approximately twice as likely as other young women to report having been pregnant.

- In a study using the data collected from the 1997 and 1999 Massachusetts YRBS, young women who had experienced dating violence were more likely than other young women to have had their first sexual experience before age 15, and did not consistently use condoms.

- In a study of 1,641 sexually active young women, those who reported physical and sexual violence were more likely to have been diagnosed with an STI or HIV than those who experienced no dating violence. Another study with 409 participants found that the young women who reported a history of abuse were about twice as likely to report having had an STI than other young women.

- In a national study, researchers found a correlation between history of physical abuse and pregnancy, and between verbal abuse and not using a condom at most recent sexual intercourse.

Many Young People Remain Silent About Dating Violence

- One study found that a young person is more likely to report abuse if they have been on five or fewer dates with the perpetrator. The longer the young person has been in the relationship, the less likely it is that he or she will report the abuse.

- Young people may remain in the abusive relationship for many reasons, including: fear of their partner, self-blame, loyalty or love for their partner, social or religious stigma, lack of understanding, the belief that dating violence is a private matter, embarrassment or denial.

- Young people under the age of 21 may not want to report the abuse if illegal alcohol consumption was involved.

Prevention Programs Can Be Successful

- Prevention programs should include education about the different forms of dating violence, understanding dynamics of power and control, early warning signs, and aspects of healthy and unhealthy relationships.

- Programs should include skills building around effective communication and conflict resolution.

- Prevention programs should address the problem of negative reproductive outcomes associated with abuse, such as STI, HIV and pregnancy, to avoid permanent consequences.

- Dating violence prevention programs should reach out to the often overlooked GLBT community.

- Programs should not only teach young people how to avoid an abusive relationship, but to also teach them how to help a friend who might be in one.

Health Care Professionals Should Screen for Abuse

- Health care professionals should not assume that patients will disclose abuse, even when asked directly.

- Health care professionals who provide sexual and reproductive health care services should routinely screen adolescents for dating violence, and should be knowledgeable about referrals and assistance in the area.

- Medical professionals and health clinics should make information about dating violence hotlines and assistance for assault patients available to all visitors.

> *"Because teen dating violence has only recently been recognized as a significant public health problem, the complex nature of this phenomenon is not fully understood."*

Teen Dating Violence Should Be Studied as an Issue Distinct from Adult Dating Violence

Carrie Mulford and Peggy C. Giordano

Carrie Mulford is a social science analyst at the National Institute of Justice and has conducted research on juvenile justice and teen dating violence. Peggy Giordano is a professor at Bowling Green State University, and her research focuses on social relationship experiences during adolescence. In the following viewpoint, Mulford and Giordano write that romantic relationships are a complex part of adolescent growth, and that abuse is a very common part of teen dating relationships. However, violence among teen partners is not adequately understood. The complexity of this issue is highlighted by the fact that although studies show that both males and females are victims of dating

Carrie Mulford and Peggy C. Giordano, "Teen Dating Violence: A Closer Look at Adolescent Romantic Relationships," *NIJ Journal*, no. 261, October 27, 2008, pp. 34–39. Copyright © 2008 by National Institute of Justice.

violence, medical practitioners report a much higher percentage of females than males as victims of dating violence among young people. Violence in teen dating relationships must be analyzed as a unique phenomenon—separate from adult intimate partner abuse—and only then will it be possible to implement effective solutions to combat teen dating violence.

As you read, consider the following questions:

1. What do the authors point out as one key difference between adolescent girls and their adult counterparts who are victimized in romantic relationships?

2. Teens who have difficulty expressing themselves sometimes resort to aggressive behaviors, state the authors of this viewpoint. What emotions do these teens have difficulty expressing? How do they express these emotions?

3. Do girls and boys exhibit similar levels of physical aggression? According to the authors, what does this mean for implementation of prevention and intervention strategies regarding teen dating violence?

Most teenagers do not experience physical aggression when they date. However, for one in 10 teens, abuse is a very real part of dating relationships.

According to the 2007 Youth Risk Behavior Survey, approximately 10 percent of adolescents nationwide reported being the victim of physical violence at the hands of a romantic partner during the previous year. The rate of psychological victimization is even higher: Between two and three in 10 reported being verbally or psychologically abused in the previous year, according to the National Longitudinal Study of Adolescent Health.

As for perpetration rates, there are currently no nationwide estimates for who does the abusing, and state estimates vary significantly. In South Carolina, for example, nearly 8 percent of adolescents reported being physically violent to a romantic partner. Interestingly, the rates of reported victimization versus perpetration in the state were similar for boys and girls. However, when it comes to severe teen dating violence—including sexual and physical assault—girls were disproportionately the victims.

The Statistics Are Confusing

At a recent workshop on teen dating violence, co-sponsored by the U.S. Department of Justice (DOJ) and Health and Human Services (HHS), researchers presented findings from several studies that found that girls and boys perpetrate the same frequency of physical aggression in romantic relationships. This finding was at odds with what practitioners attending the workshop said they encounter in their professional experience. Most of the practitioners in attendance—representing national organizations, schools and victim service community-based agencies—said that they primarily see female victims, and when they discuss teen dating violence with students, they hear that boys are the primary perpetrators.

So what *is* the reality?

Because teen dating violence has only recently been recognized as a significant public health problem, the complex nature of this phenomenon is not fully understood. Although research on rates of perpetration and victimization exists, research that examines the problem from a longitudinal perspective and considers the dynamics of teen romantic relationships is lacking. Consequently, those in the field have to rely on an *adult* framework to examine the problem of teen dating violence.

However, we find that this adult framework does not take into account key differences between adolescent and adult romantic relationships. And so, to help further the discussion, we offer in this article a gender-based analysis of teen dating violence with a developmental perspective. We look at what

we know—and what we don't know—about who is the perpetrator and who is the victim in teen dating violence. We also
discuss how adult and adolescent romantic relationships differ
in the hope that an examination of existing research will help
us better understand the problem and move the field toward
the creation of developmentally appropriate prevention programs and effective interventions for teenagers.

Victims and Perpetrators: What the Research Says

In 2001–2005, Peggy Giordano and her colleagues at Bowling
Green State University interviewed more than 1,300 seventh,
ninth and 11th graders in Toledo, Ohio. [*Editor's Note*: Giordano is one of the authors of this article.] More than half of
the girls in physically aggressive relationships said both they
and their dating partner committed aggressive acts during the
relationship. About a third of the girls said they were the sole
perpetrators, and 13 percent reported that they were the sole
victims. Almost half of the boys in physically aggressive relationships reported mutual aggression, nearly half reported
that they were the sole victim, and 6 percent reported that
they were the sole perpetrator.

These findings are generally consistent with another study
that looked at more than 1,200 Long Island, N.Y., high school
students who were currently dating. In that 2007 survey, 66
percent of boys and 65 percent of girls who were involved in
physically aggressive relationships reported mutual aggression.
Twenty-eight percent of the girls said that they were the sole
perpetrator; 5 percent said they were the sole victim. These
numbers were reversed for the boys: 5 percent said they were
the sole perpetrator; 27 percent the sole victim.

In a third study, teen couples were videotaped while per-
forming a problem-solving task. Researchers later reviewed the
tapes and identified acts of physical aggression that occurred
between the boys and girls during the exercise. They found

that 30 percent of all the participating couples demonstrated physical aggression by both partners. In 17 percent of the participating couples, only the girls perpetrated physical aggression, and in 4 percent, only the boys were perpetrators. The findings suggest that boys are less likely to be physically aggressive with a girl when someone else can observe their behavior.

Considered together, the findings from these three studies reveal that frequently there is mutual physical aggression by girls and boys in romantic relationships. However, when it comes to *motivations* for using violence and the consequences of being a victim of teen dating violence, the differences between the sexes are pronounced. Although both boys and girls report that anger is the primary motivating factor for using violence, girls also commonly report self-defense as a motivating factor, and boys also commonly cite the need to exert control. Boys are also more likely to react with laughter when their partner is physically aggressive. Girls experiencing teen dating violence are more likely than boys to suffer long-term negative behavioral and health consequences, including suicide attempts, depression, cigarette smoking and marijuana use.

Applying Adult Perspectives to Teen Dating Violence

Why do teenagers commit violence against each other in romantic relationships? We have already touched on the existing body of research on perpetration and victimization rates. Yet there is not a great deal of research that uses a longitudinal perspective or that considers the dynamics of teen romantic relationships. As a result, practitioners and researchers in the field tend to apply an adult intimate partner violence framework when examining the problem of teen dating violence.

A split currently exists, however, among experts in the adult intimate partner violence arena, and attendees at the DOJ-HHS teen dating workshop mirrored this divide.

Some experts hold that men and women are mutually combative and that this behavior should be seen as part of a larger pattern of family conflict. Supporters of this view generally cite studies that use "act" scales, which measure the number of times a person perpetrates or experiences certain acts, such as pushing, slapping or hitting. These studies tend to show that women report perpetrating slightly more physical violence than men. It is interesting to note that most studies on teen dating violence that have been conducted to date have relied primarily on "act" scales.

Another group of experts holds that men generally perpetrate serious intimate partner violence against women. They contend that men in patriarchal societies use violence to exert and maintain power and control over women. These experts also maintain that "act" scales do not accurately reflect the nature of violence in intimate relationships because they do not consider the degree of injury inflicted, coercive and controlling behaviors, the fear induced, or the context in which the acts occurred. Studies using "act" scales, they contend, lack information on power and control and emphasize the more common and relatively minor forms of aggression rather than more severe, relatively rare forms of violence in dating and intimate partner relationships. Instead, supporters of this perspective use data on injuries and in-depth interviews with victims and perpetrators.

We believe, however, that applying either of these adult perspectives to adolescents is problematic. Although both views of adult intimate partner violence can help inform our understanding of teen dating violence, it is important to consider how adolescent romantic relationships differ from adult romantic relationships in several key areas.

Who Perpetrates Teen Dating Violence?

How girls in physically aggressive relationships see it

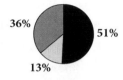

Taken From: Toledo
Adolescent Relationship
Study

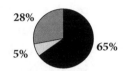

Taken From: Suffolk County
Study of Dating Aggression in
High Schools

How boys in physically aggressive relationships see it

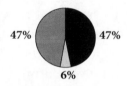

Taken From: Toledo
Adolescent Relationship
Study

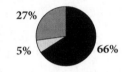

Taken From: Suffolk County
Study of Dating Aggression in
High Schools

What is observed in physically aggressive couples

Taken From: Oregon Youth
(Couples) Study

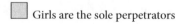

■ Mutual aggression   ▨ Girls are the sole perpetrators

▨ Boys are the sole perpetrators

Taken From: Carrie Mulford and Peggy C. Giordano, "Teen Dating
Violence: A Closer Look at Adolescent Romantic Relationships," *NIJ
Journal*, October 27, 2008.

How Teen Dating Violence Differs: Equal Power

One difference between adolescent and adult relationships is the absence of elements traditionally associated with greater male power in adult relationships. Adolescent girls are not typically dependent on romantic partners for financial stability, and they are less likely to have children to provide for and protect.

The study of seventh, ninth and 11th graders in Toledo, for example, found that a majority of the boys and girls who were interviewed said they had a relatively "equal say" in their romantic relationships. In cases in which there was a power imbalance, they were more likely to say that the female had more power in the relationship. Overall, the study found that the boys perceived that they had less power in the relationship than the girls did. Interestingly, males involved in relationships in which one or both partners reported physical aggression had a perception of less power than males in relationships without physical aggression. Meanwhile, the girls reported no perceived difference in power regardless of whether their relationships included physical aggression.

It is interesting to note that adults who perpetrate violence against family members often see themselves as powerless in their relationships. This dynamic has yet to be adequately explored among teen dating partners.

Lack of Relationship Experience

A second key factor that distinguishes violence in adult relationships from violence in adolescent relationships is the lack of experience teens have in negotiating romantic relationships. Inexperience in communicating and relating to a romantic partner may lead to the use of poor coping strategies, including verbal and physical aggression. A teen who has difficulty expressing himself or herself may turn to aggressive behaviors (sometimes in play) to show affection, frustration or jealousy.

A recent study in which boys and girls participated in focus groups on dating found that physical aggression sometimes stemmed from an inability to communicate feelings and a lack of constructive ways to deal with frustration.

As adolescents develop into young adults, they become more realistic and less idealistic about romantic relationships. They have a greater capacity for closeness and intimacy. Holding idealistic beliefs about romantic relationships can lead to disillusionment and ineffective coping mechanisms when conflict emerges. It also seems reasonable to expect that physical aggression may be more common when adolescents have not fully developed their capacity for intimacy, including their ability to communicate.

The Influence of Peers

We would be remiss to try to understand teen behavior and not consider the profound influence of friends. Peers exert more influence on each other during their adolescent years than at any other time. Research has confirmed that peer attitudes and behaviors are critical influences on teens' attitudes and behaviors related to dating violence.

Not only are friends more influential in adolescence than in adulthood, but they are also more likely to be "on the scene" and a key element in a couple's social life. In fact, roughly half of adolescent dating violence occurs when a third party is present. Relationship dynamics often play out in a very public way because teens spend a large portion of their time in school and in groups. For various reasons, a boyfriend or girlfriend may act very differently when in the presence of peers, a behavior viewed by adolescents as characteristic of an unhealthy relationship. For example, boys in one focus group study said that if a girl hit them in front of their friends, they would need to hit her back to "save face."

Conflict over how much time is spent with each other versus with friends, jealousies stemming from too much time spent with a friend of the opposite sex, and new romantic possibilities are all part of the social fabric of adolescence. Although "normal" from a developmental perspective, navigating such issues can cause conflict and, for some adolescents, lead to aggressive responses and problematic coping strategies, such as stalking, psychological or verbal abuse, and efforts to gain control.

More Research Is Needed

Adult relationships differ substantially from adolescent dating in their power dynamics, social skill development and peer influence. These factors are critical to understanding physical violence and psychological abuse in early romantic relationships and may help explain the similar perpetration rates among boys and girls suggested by current statistics.

All of this points to important implications for teen dating violence prevention and intervention strategies. Because girls engage in high levels of physical aggression and psychological abuse and most abusive relationships are characterized by mutual aggression, prevention efforts must be directed toward both males and females, and interventions for victims should include services and programming for boys and girls. Interventions must also distinguish between severe forms of violence that produce injury and fear and other more common abuse, and they must respond with appropriate safety planning, mental health services, and criminal or juvenile justice involvement.

More research on traditionally gendered relationship dynamics—and the links to relationship violence—is also needed. For instance, some male behavior may stem from an attempt to emulate other males who they believe (not always accurately, as data show) are confident and "in charge." Further, nearly one in five adolescent girls reports having sex with a partner three or more years older. These girls are at increased risk of acquiring a sexually transmitted disease because they are less likely to use a condom—possibly a result of unequal power dynamics in these relationships. This power imbalance might also increase their risk for violent victimization by older partners.

And finally, research on the extent to which teens involved in abusive relationships become involved in adult abusive relationships—whether as victims or perpetrators—is sorely needed. Many delinquent youth, for example, have a well-documented path of illegal behavior; this behavior peaks in adolescence and dramatically declines in early adulthood. A similar look at aggressive adolescent romantic relationships may help us better understand the possible progression from teen dating violence to adult intimate partner violence.

> "Confident, loving parent-child commu-
> nication leads to improved contracep-
> tive and condom use, improved com-
> munication about sex, and fewer sexual
> risk behaviors among adolescents."

Effective Parent-Teen Communication About Sex Is Critical

Nicholas Lagina and Alicia Whittaker

Nicholas Lagina and Alicia Whittaker are writers affiliated with Advocates for Youth, a website providing information on teen sexuality and related issues. In the following viewpoint, the authors stress the importance of open, positive communication between parents and teens about sex. Studies show that teens who are connected to their parents and are able to talk to them about sex tend to make better decisions about sexual activity. Although there are differences in the way parents from various races and ethnic backgrounds communicate with their children about sex, a majority of teens prefer to receive information about contra-

ception from their parents than from any other source. More effective programs are needed to help parents continue to have open, honest conversations with their teens about sexual issues.

As you read, consider the following questions:

1. What two sex-related decisions are impacted the most when parents and children have good communication about sex?

2. Which group, among Latinos, white adolescents, and African American adolescents, was most likely to report having learned "a lot" about sexual health from their parents?

3. What are the most challenging areas for parents when communicating with their teens?

When young people feel unconnected to home, family, and school, they may become involved in activities that put their health at risk. However, when parents affirm the value of their children, young people more often develop positive, healthy attitudes about themselves. Although most adults want youth to know about abstinence, contraception, and how to prevent HIV and other sexually transmitted infections (STIs), parents often have difficulty communicating about sex. Nevertheless, positive communication between parents and children greatly helps young people to establish individual values and to make healthy decisions.

Parent-Child Warmth and Communication Is Needed

A major study showed that adolescents who reported feeling connected to parents and their family were more likely than other teens to delay initiating sexual intercourse. Teens who said their families were warm and caring also reported less marijuana use and less emotional distress than their peers.

When parents and youth have good communication, along with appropriate firmness, studies have shown youth report less depression and anxiety and more self-reliance and self-esteem. They also report older age of first intercourse and lower frequency of sex during adolescence than their peers.

Lack of communication also affects behaviors and attitudes. In studies, young people who reported feeling a lack of parental warmth, love, or caring were also more likely to report emotional distress, lower self-esteem, school problems, drug use, and sexual risk behaviors.

Parent-Child Communication About Sexuality Promotes Sexually Healthy Behaviors

Confident, loving parent-child communication leads to improved contraceptive and condom use, improved communication about sex, and fewer sexual risk behaviors among adolescents.

Improved Contraception and Condom Use: In a recent study, teens who reportedly had a "good talk" with parents in the last year about sex, birth control, and the dangers of STDs [sexually transmitted diseases] were two times more likely to use condoms at the last time they had sex than teens who did not talk to their parents as often.

In one study, when mothers discussed condom use before teens initiated sexual intercourse, youth were three times more likely to use condoms than were teens whose mothers never discussed condoms or discussed condoms only after teens became sexually active. Moreover, condom use at first intercourse significantly predicted future condom use—teens who used condoms at first intercourse were 20 times more likely than other teens to use condoms regularly and 10 times more likely to use them at most recent intercourse.

Consistent users of contraception are more likely to report frequent conversations with parents than are teens who were not using contraception.

One study showed that when parents of sexually active African American and Latino youth had skilled, open, interactive discussions with their teens about sex, the youth were significantly more likely than the teens of less skilled communicators to use condoms at most recent intercourse and across time.

Improved Communication About Sex: Adolescents who have repeated communications about sex, sexuality, and development with their parents are more likely to have open and closer relationships with them, in addition to being more likely to talk with their parents in the future about sex issues than adolescents whose sexual communication with their parents included less repetition.

Teens who reported previous discussions of sexuality with parents were seven times more likely to feel able to communicate with a partner about HIV/AIDS than those who had not had such discussions with their parents.

Fewer Sexual Risk Behaviors: Two studies show that when parents make consistent efforts to know their teen's friends and whereabouts, the young people report fewer sexual partners, fewer coital acts, and more use of condoms and other forms of contraception.

Youth whose parents are open, responsive, comfortable, and confident in discussions about sex and related issues participate less often in sexual risk behavior, suggesting that the quality of communication influences the message adolescents receive about sex.

A study found that experienced African American female teens living with their mothers in a perceived supportive family were 50 percent less likely than teens in non-supportive families to report unprotected sex in the last 30 days or to report sex with a non-steady partner in the last six months. In

Parent-Teen Communication Is Limited and Often Ineffective

Parent-adolescent communication about sexuality . . . is often not very far reaching. Because most parents do not feel comfortable or competent talking with their adolescents about sexual issues, they tend to limit conversations to "safe" topics, such as developmental changes (e.g., menstruation and other pubertal changes), impersonal aspects of sexuality (e.g., reproductive facts), and negative consequences, such as AIDS and sexually transmitted diseases. . . . It is, therefore, not surprising that a significant majority of both adolescents and parents feel dissatisfied with such restricted communication about sexuality.

Steven C. Martino et al.,
"Beyond the 'Big Talk': The Roles of Breadth and Repetition
in Parent-Adolescent Communication About Sexual Topics,"
Pediatrics, *2008.*

another study of African American and Latina/Hispanic adolescent females, higher levels of mother/daughter communication about sexual risks were associated with fewer episodes of unprotected sexual intercourse.

Parent-Child Communication About Sex Varies by Race, Ethnicity, and Gender

Data has shown that 42 percent of Latino adolescents reported learning "a lot" about sexual health issues from their parents compared to 37 percent for white adolescents, but less than 60 percent of African American adolescents.

In one study, African American female adolescents reported more discussions about sex-related topics with their mothers than did male adolescents. However, males were just as likely to talk with mothers as with friends and only slightly less likely to talk with fathers.

In another study of African American and Latino adolescents, a significantly greater percentage of Latino teens than African American teens reported discussing at least two sex-related topics—HIV/AIDS and choosing a sex partner—with their father. Latino teens were also twice as likely as African American teens to discuss choosing a sex partner with their mothers.

Research shows that parents are the preferred source of information about contraception: 19.2 percent of students said they would prefer to get information about contraception from their parents rather than from community health centers, classes, hospitals, private doctors, television, or friends (12.5, 12.0, 11.1, 8.8, 7.9, and 6.9 percent, respectively).

Negative or No Communication Can Lead to Negative Results

In studies, young people who reported feeling a lack of parental warmth, love, or caring were also more likely to report emotional distress, lower self-esteem, school problems, drug use, and sexual risk behaviors.

One study of urban African American and Latino mothers and their pre-teen and early adolescent daughters found many mothers reluctant to discuss more than biological issues and negative consequences of sexual activity. Maternal communications about sex, often restrictive and moralistic in tone, deterred daughters from confiding in their mothers. Daughters, in reaction, sometimes became secretly involved in romantic relationships.

The National Longitudinal Study of Adolescent Health found that Latina and Asian mothers were less likely to talk to their children about sex, but most likely to accurately report their daughters' sexual status, whereas the opposite was true for African Americans.

Parents Play an Important Role, but Need Resources and Support

Studies show that many parents face challenges in being prepared to have discussions with young people about relationships, development, and sex. Schools are an important partner in helping young people prevent negative sexual health outcomes through comprehensive sex education.

Many parents are not able to provide all the information about sex that young people need. In one survey, only 38 percent of young women and 25 percent of young men said they had ever gotten a good idea from their parents that helped them talk about sexual issues with their girlfriend/boyfriend.

One study of 192 college student participants showed that 77 percent of their mothers engaged in some level of sexuality communication with them compared to only 37 percent of their fathers.

In a recent poll, 89 percent of Americans said it is important for sex education in schools to include information about contraception and preventing unintended pregnancy and sexually transmitted infections, including HIV.

Even though parents are the primary source of information about sexual and reproductive health for their children, few effective programs that help parents positively influence their children's sexual behavior exist. More research into science-driven, skills-based programs to support parent-child communication is needed.

Periodical and Internet Sources Bibliography

The following articles have been selected to supplement the diverse views presented in this chapter.

Sakeena Abdulraheem	"Teen Dating Violence in the Muslim Community: Protecting the Family, Eradicating Hopelessness, and Healing the Community," Faith Trust Institute, 2010. www.faithtrust institute.org.
Laura Alspaugh	"Teen Dating Violence," July 16, 2009. www.livestrong.com.
Centers for Disease Control and Prevention	"Understanding Teen Dating Violence Fact Sheet," 2010. www.cdc.gov/violenceprevention.
Alicia Chang	"Teen Sex Not Always Bad for School Performance," *The Huffington Post*, August 15, 2010. www.huffingtonpost.com.
Sinikka Elliot	"My Kid Wouldn't Do That," *States News Service*, May 3, 2010.
Andrea Gordon	"What Sex Ed Never Taught Your Kids," *Toronto Star*, November 19, 2009.
Robert Rector	"Teen Pregnancy: Bogus Problem, Bogus Solution," *National Review Online*, January 27, 2010.
Hope Riccciotti and Kate Adelstein	"Teen Pregnancy Rate Rising for First Time in 15 Years," *Boston Banner*, February 12, 2009.
Amy Kossoff Smith	"Sexting: How Parents Can Keep Kids Safe," *The Monitor* (McAllen, Texas), May 4, 2009.
Martha Waggoner	"Parents Don't Believe Their Kids Have Sex," *Associated Press Newswire*, June 16, 2010.

OPPOSING
VIEWPOINTS®
SERIES

CHAPTER 3

How Should Society Educate Teens About Sex?

Chapter Preface

In April 2010, two secondary schools in Dundee, Scotland, approved an expenditure of £45,000 to launch a peer-led sex education program in middle and high school. The goal was to reinforce the message of safe sex. The decision set off a firestorm of debate about the efficacy of peer-led sex education programs. Proponents argued that peer-led sex education programs are more effective and provide teens with opportunities to communicate openly about issues regarding sex. Opponents stated that peers are not qualified to handle issues pertaining to sexuality and should not have to shoulder a burden they are ill-equipped to handle.

Prevention of pregnancy, reduction of sexually transmitted diseases (STDs), and disseminating information on contraceptives are major goals of all comprehensive sex education programs. However, there is no consensus among American parents, legislators, and educators about the best and most effective way to deliver this information to teens. Peer-led sex education programs are thus part of a larger debate in American society about the best way to educate teens about sex. Peer-led sex education programs have many detractors in the United States. Many adults argue that peer-led sex education programs are unable to handle issues pertaining to sex in a way that is effectively preventative. In contrast, teens asked about the efficacy of peer-led programs on the website Sex, Etc. were much more receptive to the idea of talking about sex to a peer rather than an adult. Many teens expressed appreciation about their peer counselor's willingness to discuss sex and contraception, versus adult counselors who, reported the teens, tend to stress abstinence and delayed sexual activity.

In contrast to the United States, other countries are much more receptive to the idea of peer-led sex education programs. For example, in a 2004 article posted on SexualHealth

.com, Judith Stephenson wrote about the success of such programs in China, noting that the programs allowed Chinese youth to "speak out openly to knowledgeable peers about the very sensitive issue of sex." Avert.org, the website for AVERT, a UK-based organization that works to minimize the spread of HIV and AIDS across the world, cites several programs in countries like Thailand, Australia, India, Cameroon, and several West African nations where peer-led sex education programs have proven effective in disseminating information about HIV, AIDS and other sexually transmitted diseases. Avert.org notes in several articles on sex education that the common ground shared by peer educators and their target populations is a significant factor in the ability to effectively and openly discuss sensitive issues related to sexuality.

In the case of the United States in particular, Avert.org cites examples where peer-led sex education among teens from minority populations, specifically black Americans, has had a positive impact on reducing teen pregnancies. Proponents of peer-led sex education in the United States argue that teens are much more likely to heed messages from peers about the use of contraceptives and are more willing to discuss these issues openly with their peers instead of adults. Websites such as Sex, Etc. are based on this premise, and teens who contact the site with questions chat with trained teen counselors who are supervised by adult personnel. However, peer-led sex education programs for teens have not met with success in school settings. One reason for this, states an article on Avert.org titled "Sex Education That Works," is that American teen counselors tend to belong to a different peer group than their target populations. American teen counselors tend to be highly motivated and academically oriented kids, versus their clients, who tend to belong to lower-income families and are often academically low-performing. Many teens who want answers about sex, especially as it relates to sexual orientation issues, hesitate to bring them to the attention of their peers because they fear exposure.

The anonymity of online communication alleviates such concerns. Questions posed by teens to their peers online are much more frank than the ones they direct to teachers, parents, or even peers in face-to-face encounters. For example, specific questions about penis size, breast size and shape, and the like, while not necessarily the most critical issues that need to be addressed by sex education, are common on teen-run websites. In such cases, teens are able to get accurate factual information that they may not be able to access under other circumstances.

The controversy about peer-led sex education is part of a larger debate about the most effective way to talk to teens about sex. In the viewpoints in the following chapter, commentators offer differing opinions on the best way to educate teens about sex.

> "School-based [sex] education programs are particularly good at providing information and opportunities for skills development and attitude clarification in more formal ways, through lessons within a curriculum."

Schools, Parents, and Communities Should Contribute to Educating Teens About Sex

Grace Chen

Grace Chen writes for Public School Review, an online resource with information on American public schools and their surrounding communities. In this viewpoint, Chen explains that rising teen pregnancy rates among American teens has prompted parents and school administrators to concede the importance of sex education provided by schools. Although there are many avenues to impart information about sex to teens, research shows that school-based sex education programs provide one of the best ways to convey sexual health information to adolescents. It is easy for parents to monitor sex education materials being shared

with their children in school, Chen asserts, and parents can use
these resources at home to reinforce information taught at school.

As you read, consider the following questions:

1. With increased funding for sex education, what goal
   does the federal government hope to achieve?

2. According to a source cited in this viewpoint, what are
   the benefits of community-based sex education projects?

3. According to Avert, how can schools help to get parents
   involved in their children's sex education?

According to statistics compiled by the Guttmacher Institute, the US has "one of the highest teen pregnancy rates
in the developed world—almost twice as high as those of England, Wales and Canada, and eight times as high as those of
the Netherlands and Japan." Because of the rising pregnancy
rates among teens, in addition to the rising rates of sexual activity among teens, both parents and public schools are exploring the best sex education programs to benefit students.

While sex education has historically brought forth great
tension and debate between schools and communities, National Public Radio [NPR] asserts that "providing effective sex
education can seem daunting because it means tackling potentially sensitive issues. However, because sex education com-
prises many individual activities, which take place across a
wide range of settings and periods of time, there are lots of
opportunities to contribute."

The Debate of Sex Education in Public Schools

While some Americans express mixed opinions on *how* public
schools should teach sex education courses, NPR reports that
the once heated debate over whether or not schools should
even teach teens about sex has now dwindled: "A new poll by

NPR, the Kaiser Family Foundation, and Harvard's Kennedy School of Government finds that only 7 percent of Americans say sex education should not be taught in schools. Moreover, in most places there is even little debate about what *kind* of sex education should be taught, although there are still pockets of controversy."

According to NPR, debates between schools and parents has dwindled, as more community members are becoming both informed and involved in the discussion of sex education in schools: today, surveys reveal there is "little serious conflict over sex education in their communities nowadays. Nearly three-quarters of the principals (74 percent) say there have been no recent discussions or debate in PTA [parent teacher association], school board or other public meetings about what to teach in sex ed. Likewise, few principals report being contacted by elected officials."

Sex Education and the Federal Government

According to NPR, while the majority of Americans agree that teens *should* learn about sex in public schools, many individuals are conflicted on the methods of teaching, as 15% of Americans argue that schools should only teach abstinence from sexual intercourse, while further asserting that schools should not provide information on how to obtain and use various modes of contraception.

Added to this, however, approximately 46% of Americans believe that both abstinence and contraception should be taught in schools. While this conflict wages forward, federal funds are currently being made to support abstinence-based programs in public schools. As NPR reveals, "in his [2008] State of the Union address President [George W.] Bush called for an increase in the funding."

To navigate this issue of teaching students to make the best decisions, The Heritage Foundation asserts that the federal government's new regulation of funds, allocated to sex education in schools and communities, can provide individuals with more opportunities to become informed about good decisions and safety.

As The Heritage Foundation explains, "government-funded contraceptive programs promote the use of contraception for two purposes: to prevent unwanted pregnancy and to reduce the risk of infection by sexually transmitted diseases (STDs). To meet these goals, government contraceptive programs may provide contraceptive services, promote and encourage contraceptive use, or both." As government funding is increasing for sex education and programs for teens, federal support is aimed at the goal of fostering safe sex and comprehensive programs based on [the] lessons [of] abstinence, protection, and prevention.

Revised Programs and Opportunities for Support

As social norms among teens shift, communities are finding new ways to proactively educate teens on sex education issues. As NPR explains, "Because sex education can take place across a wide range of settings, there are lots of opportunities to contribute."

Foremost, parental involvement is considered to be the best resource for students to receive ongoing individual support and information early in their lives. Added to this, "school-based education programs are particularly good at providing information and opportunities for skills development and attitude clarification in more formal ways, through lessons within a curriculum."

Yet parents and schools do not have to bear the brunt of continuing the discussion with teens [says NPR]:

Community-based projects provide opportunities for young people to access advice and information in less formal ways. Sexual health and other health and welfare services can provide access to specific information, support and advice. Sex education through the mass media, often supported by lo-

Effective Sex Education

The most effective sex education acknowledges the different contributions each setting can make. School programs, which involve parents, notifying them what is being taught and when, can support the initiation of dialogue at home. Parents and schools both need to engage with young people about the messages that they get from the media, and give them opportunities for discussion.

In some countries, the involvement of young people themselves in developing and providing sex education has increased as a means of ensuring the relevance and accessibility of provision. Consultation with young people at the point when programmes are designed, helps ensure that they are relevant and the involvement of young people in delivering programmes may reinforce messages as they model attitudes and behaviour to their peers.

School-based sex education can be an important and effective way of enhancing young people's knowledge, attitudes and behaviour. There is widespread agreement that formal education should include sex education and what works has been well-researched.

"Sex Education That Works,"
Avert, June 10, 2009.

cal, regional or national government and non-governmental agencies and departments, can help to raise public awareness of sex health issues.

As NPR further explains, in bringing together and joining these separate elements, teens can be provided with an ongoing coherency in their overall education—and specifically in the realm of sexual education.

Specific Parental Involvement Strategies

Since parents have the longest and most ongoing influence on a child's life, parents can be involved in the decision making processes of schools by meeting with teachers, attending open-forum school board meetings, and by being involved in parent programs like the PTA/PTSA [parent teacher student association].

As Avert, a program dedicated to educating both teens and adults about safe sex, supports, "The most effective sex education acknowledges the different contributions each setting can make. School programs that involve parents, notifying them what is being taught and when, can support the initiation of dialogue at home. Parents and schools both need to engage with young people about the messages that they get from the media, and give them opportunities for discussion."

Parents can find out about their school and community's specific sex education program by checking their community's individual curriculum standards, available for all individuals online. Paired with this, schools often send home rubrics and information on the content of courses; as such, parents can monitor their child's classroom content by using such resources as opportunities to become more informed and involved in their child's learning process.

| "Authentic abstinence programs are . . . crucial to efforts aimed at reducing unwed childbearing and improving youth well-being."

Abstinence-Only Education Programs Are Effective

Christine C. Kim and Robert Rector

Christine C. Kim is a policy analyst and Robert Rector is a senior research fellow at The Heritage Foundation. In the following viewpoint, they present evidence that abstinence education is the best way for teens to delay sexual activity. They examine numerous studies of abstinence education as well as several studies of virginity pledge programs, explaining that such studies showed positive results. According to the authors, abstinent teens are, on the whole, better adjusted socially and academically, with significantly reduced rates of sexually transmitted diseases and out-of-wedlock pregnancies.

As you read, consider the following questions:

1. According to the authors, what are three types of benefits stressed by abstinence education programs?

2. How many studies of abstinence education do the authors cite? Of these, how many studies reported positive outcomes? What are two major results of abstinence education programs cited by the authors?

3. In the authors' view, how does the government implicitly support messages of sexual permissiveness?

Teen sexual activity remains a widespread problem confronting the nation. Each year, some 2.6 million teenagers become sexually active—a rate of 7,000 teens per day. Among high school students, nearly half report having engaged in sexual activity, and one-third are currently active.

Sexual activity during teenage years poses serious health risks for youths and has long-term implications. Early sexual activity is associated with an increased risk of sexually transmitted diseases (STDs), reduced psychological and emotional well-being, lower academic achievement, teen pregnancy, and out-of-wedlock childbearing. Many of these risks are avoidable if teens choose to abstain from sexual activity. Abstinence is the surest way to avoid the risk of STDs and unwed childbearing.

Abstinence education [as explained in section 510(b) of the Social Security Act] "teaches abstinence from sexual activity outside marriage as the expected standard for all school age children" and stresses the social, psychological, and health benefits of abstinence. Abstinence programs also provide youths with valuable life and decision-making skills that lay the foundation for personal responsibility and developing healthy relationships and marriages later in life. These programs emphasize preparing young people for future-oriented goals.

Abstinence Results in Many Benefits

Studies have shown that abstinent teens report, on average, better psychological well-being and higher academic achievement than those who are sexually active. Delaying the initiation of or reducing early sexual activity among teens can decrease their overall exposure to risks of unwed childbearing, STDs, and psycho-emotional harm. Authentic abstinence programs are therefore crucial to efforts aimed at reducing unwed childbearing and improving youth well-being.

Opponents of abstinence education contend that these programs fail to influence teen sexual behavior. At this stage, the available evidence supports neither this assessment nor the wholesale dismissal of authentic abstinence education programs.

Studies of Abstinence Education

This paper discusses 21 studies of abstinence education. Fifteen studies examined abstinence programs that were primarily intended to teach abstinence. Of these 15 studies, 11 reported positive findings. The other six studies analyzed virginity pledges, and of these six studies, five reported positive findings. Overall, 16 of the 21 studies reported statistically significant positive results, such as delayed sexual initiation and reduced levels of early sexual activity, among youths who have received abstinence education. Five studies did not report any significant positive results. . . .

While abstinence programs emphasize the message of abstinence until marriage as the standard for all school-age children, simply delaying the initiation or reducing current levels of sexual activity among teens can decrease teens' overall exposure to the risk of physical and psycho-emotional harm. . . .

Reasons of the Heart

Taught over 20 class periods by certified and program-trained health educators, the Reasons of the Heart (ROH) curriculum focuses on individual character development and teaches adolescents the benefits that are associated with abstinence until marriage.

A 2008 study evaluated the ROH curriculum's impact on adolescent sexual activity among seventh grade students in three suburban northern Virginia public schools. The researchers also collected data on a comparison group of seventh grade students in two nearby middle schools that did not participate in the program. Students in those schools instead received the state's standard family life education, which included two videos on HIV/STD prevention and one on abstinence.

The evaluators surveyed seventh grade students in all five schools before and after the program. They found that, a year after the program, 32 (9.2 percent) of the 347 ROH students who were virgins at the initial survey had initiated sexual activity, compared with 31 (or 16.4 percent) of the 189 comparison group students. Controlling for the differences between the comparison group and ROH students, the study reported that ROH students were half as likely as comparison group students to initiate sexual activity. The evaluators concluded, "This result appears to compare favorably to the reductions in initiation achieved by some of the abstinence programs [evaluated in earlier studies]."

Sex Can Wait

Sex Can Wait is a three-series abstinence education program with one series for upper-elementary students, a second for middle school students, and a third for high school students. The Sex Can Wait program lasts five weeks and offers lessons on character building, important life skills, and reproductive biology.

A 2006 study evaluated the program's long-term (18-month) impact on adolescent sexual behavior. The researchers compared students who participated in Sex Can Wait to those who received their school districts' standard sex education curricula on two behavioral outcomes: overall abstinence and abstinence during the last 30 days. As the authors noted, "the study compared the effects of the Sex Can Wait curriculum to 'current practice' rather than true 'control conditions.'"

The researchers found that, 18 months after the program, upper-elementary students who participated in Sex Can Wait were less likely than non-participants to report engaging in recent sexual activity. Among middle school students, participants were also less likely than non-participants to report engaging in sexual activity ever and in the preceding month before the 18-month follow-up. Finally, among high school students, the authors found reduced levels of sexual activity in the short term but not in the 18-month follow-up.

Heritage Keepers

Heritage Keepers is a primary prevention abstinence program for middle school and high school students. The program offers an interactive three-year, two-level curriculum.

To assess Heritage Keepers' impact, a group of evaluators compared some 1,200 virgin students who attended schools that faithfully implemented the program to some 250 students in demographically and geographically comparable schools who did not receive the abstinence intervention. One year after the program, 14.5 percent of Heritage Keepers students had become sexually active compared with 26.5 percent of the comparison group.

Overall, Heritage Keepers students "were about one-half as likely" as comparison group students to initiate sex after adjusting for pre-program differences between the two groups. The study found similar results in subsets of African-American students, Caucasian students, boys, and girls.

For Keeps

A study published in 2005 evaluated the For Keeps curriculum as implemented in five urban and two suburban middle schools in the Midwest. Schools were assigned by the school

Abstinence-Only Intervention Can Be Effective

While the results do not always clearly favor abstinence education, this graph shows that theory-based abstinence-only intervention can result in an overall reduction in self-reported sexual activity at baseline and in follow-up visits for several months afterwards. Participants in the program were African American students ages 11 and 12. They were divided into several groups to receive different levels or types of sex education. Programs included at 12-hour (12-hr) and an 8-hour (8-hr) comprehensive curriculum that addressed sexual intercourse and condom use, an 8-hour safer sex-only curriculum that targeted increased condom use, an 8-hour abstinence-only curriculum, and a health control curriculum that targeted health issues unrelated to sexual behavior.

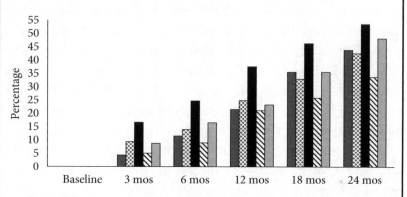

Respondents reporting on whether they have ever had sexual intercourse*

*Excludes participants who reported sexual intercourse at baseline

 12-hr comprehensive

8-hr comprehensive

Safer sex only

Abstinence only

Health control

Taken From: John B. Jemmott, III, Loretta S. Jemmott, and Geoffrey T. Fong. "Efficacy of a Theory-Based Abstinence-Only Intervention Over 24 Months: A Randomized Controlled Trial With Young Adolescents," *Archives of Pediatrics & Adolescent Medicine*, 2010.

districts to receive the program, which was part of a county-wide teen pregnancy prevention initiative.

Taught by outside facilitators, For Keeps was a five-day curriculum with 40-minute sessions that focused on character development and the benefits of abstinence and tried to help students understand how pregnancy and sexually transmitted diseases can impede their long-term goals. It also emphasized the psycho-emotional and economic consequences of early sexual activity. The curriculum was intended both for students who had become sexually active and for those who had not.

The evaluation collected data on all students through a pretest survey, and some 2,000 youths (about 70 percent of those who took the pretest survey) responded to a follow-up survey conducted about five months after the program ended. Among youths who engaged in any sexual behavior during the follow-up period, some who participated in For Keeps reported a reduction in "the amount of casual sex, as evidenced by fewer episodes of sex and fewer sexual partners" during the evaluation period, although program participants did not differ from non-participants in the likelihood of engaging in sexual activity during the follow-up interval.

Best Friends

The Best Friends (BF) program began in 1987 and operates in about 90 schools across the United States. The Best Friends curriculum is an abstinence-based character-building program for girls starting in the sixth grade and offers a variety of services such as group discussions, mentoring, and community activities. Discussion topics include friendship, love and dating, self-respect, decision making, alcohol and drug abuse, physical fitness and nutrition, and AIDS/STDs. The curriculum's predominant theme is encouraging youths to abstain from high-risk behaviors and sexual activity.

A 2005 study evaluated the District of Columbia's Best Friends program, which operated in six of the District's 20 middle schools. The study compared data on BF participants to data from the Youth Risk Behavior Surveys (YRBS) conducted for the District. When the authors of the study compared Best Friends schools to District schools that did not have the program, they found that Best Friends schools tended to be located in the more disadvantaged sections of the city and were academically comparable to or slightly worse than the District's middle schools in general.

Adjusting for the survey year, students' age, grade, and race and ethnicity, the study reported that Best Friends girls were nearly 6.5 times more likely to abstain from sexual activity than YRBS respondents. They were 2.4 times more likely to abstain from smoking, 8.1 times more likely to abstain from illegal drug use, and 1.9 times more likely to abstain from drinking.

Not Me, Not Now

Not Me, Not Now, a community-wide abstinence intervention program, targeted children ages nine through 14 in Monroe County, New York, which includes the city of Rochester. The Not Me, Not Now program devised a mass communications strategy to promote the abstinence message through paid television and radio advertising, billboards, posters distributed in schools, educational materials for parents, an interactive Web site, and educational sessions in school and community settings. The program had five objectives: raising awareness of the problem of teen pregnancy, increasing understanding of the negative consequences of teen pregnancy, developing resistance to peer pressure, promoting parent-child communication, and promoting abstinence among teens.

Not Me, Not Now was effective in reaching early teens, with some 95 percent of the target audience in the county reporting that they had seen a Not Me, Not Now ad. During the intervention period, there was a statistically significant positive shift in attitudes among pre-teens and early teens in the county.

The sexual activity rate of 15-year-olds across the county dropped by a statistically significant amount, from 46.6 percent to 31.6 percent, during this period. The pregnancy rate for girls ages 15 through 17 in Monroe County fell by a statistically significant amount, from 63.4 pregnancies per 1,000 girls to 49.5 pregnancies per 1,000. The teen pregnancy rate fell more rapidly in Monroe County than in comparison counties and upstate New York in general, and the differences in the rates of decrease were statistically significant.

Abstinence by Choice

Abstinence by Choice operated in 20 schools in the Little Rock area of Arkansas. The program targeted seventh, eighth, and ninth grade students and reached about 4,000 youths each year. The curriculum included a five-day workshop with speakers, presentations, skits, videos, and an adult mentoring component.

A 2001 evaluation analyzed a sample of 329 students and found that only 5.9 percent of eighth grade girls who had participated in Abstinence by Choice a year earlier had initiated sexual activity compared with 10.2 percent of non-participants. Among eighth grade boy participants, 15.8 percent had initiated sexual activity, compared with 22.8 percent among non-participating boys. (The sexual activity rate of students in the program was compared with the rate of sexual activity among control students in the same grade and schools prior to commencement of the program.)

HIV Risk-Reduction Intervention

A 1998 study evaluated a two-day abstinence-based HIV risk-reduction intervention. The program was delivered to some 200 African-American middle school students in Philadelphia. Students volunteered to participate in a weekend health promotion program, and the volunteers were then randomly assigned to an abstinence education program, a safer-sex education program, or a regular health program (the control group) delivered by trained adult and peer (high school student) facilitators.

The researchers found that, during the three-month follow-up, students in the abstinence programs were less likely to report having engaged in recent sexual activity compared with students in the control group and that they were marginally less likely to report having engaged in recent sexual activity compared to students in the safer-sex program.

Although the three groups generally did not differ in their reports of sexual activity in the preceding three months during the six-month and 12-month follow-ups, the researchers did report that, among students who had sexual experience before the intervention, those in the safer-sex group reported fewer days of sexual activity on average than students in the control group and the abstinence group reported.

Stay SMART

Delivered to Boys and Girls Clubs of America participants, Stay SMART integrated abstinence education with substance-use prevention and incorporated instructions on general life skills as well. The 12-session curriculum, led by Boys and Girls Club staff, used a postponement approach to early sexual activity and targeted both sexually experienced and sexually inexperienced adolescents. Participation in Boys and Girls Clubs and Stay SMART was voluntary.

A 1995 study evaluated Stay SMART's impact on adolescent sexual behavior. The study measured the sexual attitudes and behavior of more than 200 youths who participated in Stay SMART or Stay SMART plus the boosters and compared their outcomes to some 100 youths who did not participate in Stay SMART but were still involved in the Boys and Girls Clubs. The analysis controlled for demographic and baseline characteristics to test for the program's independent effect on adolescent sexual behavior and attitudes.

The study found that, two years after the program, youths who had engaged in prior sexual activity and participated in the stand-alone Stay SMART program exhibited reduced levels of recent sexual activity compared with non-participants and, interestingly, participants in the Stay SMART-plus-boosters program as well. Among participants who were virgins prior to the program, the study did not find a statistically significant program effect.

Project Taking Charge

Project Taking Charge was a six-week abstinence curriculum delivered in home economics classes during the school year. It was designed for use in low-income communities with high rates of teen pregnancy. The curriculum contained elements on self-development; basic information about sexual biology (e.g., anatomy, physiology, and pregnancy); vocational goal-setting; family communication; and values instruction on the importance of delaying sexual activity until marriage.

The program was evaluated in Wilmington, Delaware, and West Point, Mississippi, based on a small sample of 91 adolescents. Control and experimental groups were created by randomly assigning classrooms either to receive or not to receive the program. The students were assessed immediately before and after the program and at a six-month follow-up. In the six-month follow-up, Project Taking Charge was shown to have had a statistically significant effect in increasing adolescents' knowledge of the problems associated with teen pregnancy, the problems of sexually transmitted diseases, and reproductive biology.

The program may also have delayed the onset of sexual activity among some of the participants. About 23 percent of participants who were virgins at the pretest initiated sexual activity during the follow-up interval, compared with 50 percent of the youths in the control group, although the authors urged caution in interpreting these numbers due to the small sample size.

Teen-Aid and Sex Respect

An evaluation of the Teen-Aid and Sex Respect abstinence programs in three Utah school districts reported that certain groups of youths who received these programs delayed the initiation of sexual activity. To determine the effects of the programs, students in schools with the abstinence programs were compared with students in similar control schools within the same school districts. Statistical adjustments were applied to control for any initial differences between program participants and control group students.

In the aggregate sample, the researchers did not find any differences in the rates of sexual initiation between youths who had received abstinence education and those who had not. However, analyzing a cohort of high school students who had fairly permissive attitudes, they found that program participants were one-third less likely to engage in sexual activity one year after the programs compared with non-participants (22.4 percent versus 37 percent).

Even when the researchers adjusted for students' dating and drinking behavior, religious involvement, family composition, peer pressure, and other factors, the differences between the two groups remained statistically significant. (Statistically significant changes in behavior were not found among a similar group of junior high school students.) The researchers found it notable that youths who had more permissive attitudes were [as written by Stan E. Weed et al.] "not only receptive and responsive to the abstinence message in the short run, but that some influence on behavior [was] also occurring."

Virginity Pledge Studies Yielded Positive Results

Using the National Longitudinal Study of Adolescent Health (Add Health), a nationally representative sample of American youth, several studies have found that adolescent virginity pledging was associated with delayed or reduced levels of teen sexual activity, other risky behaviors, teen pregnancy, and STDs.

Delayed Sexual Activity. A 1997 study published in the *Journal of the American Medical Association* examined a large national sample of teenagers in the seventh through 12th grades. The study compared students who had taken a formal virginity pledge with students who had not taken a pledge but were otherwise identical in race, income, school performance, degree of religiousness, and other social and demographic factors. Based on this analysis, the authors found that the level of sexual activity among students who had taken a formal pledge of virginity was one-fourth the level of their counterparts who had not taken a pledge. The researchers [Michael Resnick et al.] also noted that "[a]dolescents who reported having taken a pledge to remain a virgin were at significantly lower risk of early age of sexual debut."

Another study of the virginity pledge movement, published in 2001, found a similar association between pledging and delayed sexual activity. According to the authors [Peter S. Bearman and Hanna Brückner]:

> Adolescents who pledge, controlling for all of the usual characteristics of adolescents and their social contexts that are associated with the transition to sex, are much less likely than adolescents who do not pledge, to have intercourse. The delay effect is substantial and robust. Pledging delays intercourse for a long time.

Based on a sample of more than 5,000 students, the study reported that taking a virginity pledge was associated with a reduction of approximately one-third in the likelihood of early sexual activity, adjusted for a host of other factors linked to sexual activity rates including gender, age, physical maturity, parental disapproval of sexual activity, school achievement, and race. When taking a virginity pledge was combined with strong parental disapproval of sexual activity, the probability of initiating sexual activity was reduced by 75 percent or more. The authors did note that the pledge effect depended on youths' age and their peer group context.

Life Outcomes in Young Adulthood. By the third wave of the Add Health survey, administered in 2001, respondents had reached young adulthood, ranging between 19 and 25 years of age. In some cases, the virginity pledge may have been taken up to seven years earlier. Nonetheless, for many respondents, the delaying effect associated with pledging during adolescence appeared to last into young adulthood.

Analyzing the most recent Add Health data, a 2004 study found that adolescent virginity pledging was linked to a number of positive life outcomes. For example, a 22-year-old white female pledger from an intact family with median levels of family income, academic performance, self-esteem, and religious observance was two-thirds less likely to become pregnant before age 18 and 40 percent less likely to have a birth out of wedlock compared with a non-pledger with identical characteristics. Strong pledgers with the same characteristics were 40 percent less likely to initiate sexual activity before age 18 and had an average of one-third fewer sexual partners compared with non-pledgers with the same demographic profile.

STDs and Risky Sexual Behaviors. Analyzing the same sample of respondents, another study found that virginity pledging during adolescence was also associated with lower rates of STD infection among young adults. The STD rate among pledgers averaged 25 percent lower than the rate of non-pledgers of the same age, gender, race, family background, and religiosity. Significantly, the study found that virginity pledging was a stronger predictor of STD reduction than condom use on five different measures of STDs.

The protective effect of pledging may have extended to other behaviors as well. According to a 2005 study, young adults who took a virginity pledge during adolescence were less likely to engage in a number of risky sexual behaviors compared with those who did not take a pledge. . . .

Abstinence Education Does Work

Today's young people face strong peer pressure to engage in risky behavior and must navigate media and popular culture that endorse and even glamorize permissiveness and casual sex. Alarmingly, the government implicitly supports these messages by spending over $1 billion each year promoting contraception and safe-sex education—12 times what it spends on abstinence education.

Although 80 percent of parents want schools to teach youths to abstain from sexual activity until they are in a committed adult romantic relationship nearing marriage—the core message of abstinence education—these parental values are rarely communicated in the classroom.

In the classroom, the prevailing mentality often condones teen sexual activity as long as youths use contraceptives. Abstinence is usually mentioned only in passing, if at all. Sadly, many teens who need to learn about the benefits of abstaining from sexual activity during the teenage years never hear them, and many students who choose to abstain fail to receive adequate support for their decisions.

Teen sexual activity is costly, not just for teens, but also for society. Teens who engage in sexual activity risk a host of negative outcomes including STD infection, emotional and psychological harm, lower educational attainment, and out-of-wedlock childbearing.

Genuine abstinence education is therefore crucial to the physical and psycho-emotional well-being of the nation's youth. In addition to teaching the benefits of abstaining from sexual activity until marriage, abstinence programs focus on developing character traits that prepare youths for future-oriented goals.

When considering federal funding for abstinence education programs and reauthorization of Title V abstinence education programs, including maintaining the current definition of "abstinence education," lawmakers should consider *all* of the available empirical evidence.

> "A systematic look at the federal abstinence-only effort concluded in 2007 that none of the programs it evaluated were effective in stopping or even delaying sex."

Abstinence-Only Sex Education Programs Are Ineffective

Heather D. Boonstra

Heather D. Boonstra is a senior policy associate with the Guttmacher Institute; she works to promote the institute's sexual and reproductive health agenda in federal law and policy. In the following viewpoint, Boonstra argues that the time for abstinence-only education programs is past—instead, policy makers need to support funding initiatives that take a more comprehensive approach to sex education. According to the author, abstinence-only programs have failed to demonstrate any significant impact on teen sexual behavior. Further, many of these programs withhold important medical information from adolescents, leaving them ill-equipped to handle health- and life-saving decisions.

As you read, consider the following questions:

1. Which leading health professional groups have raised concerns about government support of abstinence-only education programs? What is their main concern regarding government support of these programs?

2. How many states have opted to decline applications for funding that supports abstinence education grants?

3. In addition to delaying or reducing sexual activity, what does the author cite as other positive outcomes that result from comprehensive sex education programs?

In the weeks since he was sworn into office [in 2009], speculation has continued around the new directions in which President Barack Obama, with the help of a more supportive Congress, might take the country. For opponents of sex education programs that focus exclusively on abstinence, there is already a feeling of the beginning of a new era. Under the [George W.] Bush administration and with the strong support of congressional social conservatives, "abstinence-only-until-marriage" emerged as the sanctioned approach to reducing U.S. teen pregnancy and sexually transmitted infection (STI) rates. Since 1996, well over $1 billion in federal and mandatory state matching grants has been spent to promote premarital abstinence among young Americans, through highly restrictive programs that ignore or often actively denigrate the effectiveness of contraceptives and safer-sex behaviors.

At long last, however, the tide seems to be turning. Over the last several years, the case against abstinence-only education has mounted. Continued funding for federal abstinence-only programs was hotly debated during a hearing held before the House Committee on Oversight and Government Reform in April 2008. At this first-ever congressional hearing to examine the effectiveness of abstinence-only education, social conservatives were on the defensive against a wealth of evidence that such a highly restrictive educational approach does not work to stop or even materially delay teen sex. A panel of public health experts, including representatives of the American Public Health Association, the Academy of Pediatrics and the Institute of Medicine, testified that there is no evidence base to support the current massive federal investment in abstinence-only programs.

Later that year, Congress rejected President Bush's request for yet another significant increase for the abstinence-only program and declined to give it any increase. Now, opponents of abstinence-only education are taking the next step, calling on the Obama administration and Congress to end federal funding for such programs entirely. Instead, they say, policymakers should throw their support behind a more comprehensive approach to sex education that genuinely addresses the reality of young people's lives—education that helps youth to delay sexual activity, even as it equips them with the information and skills they will need to behave safely and responsibly when they do begin to have sex.

The Rise of Abstinence-Only Programs

Only a few decades ago, debate over sex education focused on whether public schools had a role at all in educating children and young people about sex-related matters or whether parents should be the sole transmitter of sexually related values and information to their children. However, as the level of concern over teenage pregnancy—and later AIDS—increased, so did public support for sex education in schools. Over a few years in the 1970s and 1980s, the number of states that had policies requiring or encouraging the teaching of sex education grew rapidly.

Having lost the debate over whether there should be sex education in schools, groups that once opposed school-based programs moved to a new strategy—one aimed at limiting the content of programs to the promotion of premarital abstinence. In 1981, the first grants for what later came to be called "abstinence-only" programs were authorized under the Adolescent Family Life Act (AFLA). Sponsored by congressional family planning opponents, AFLA was promoted as a "family-centered" alternative to contraceptive counseling and services to teenagers; instead, this program's stated goal was to promote premarital "chastity and self-discipline."

Although AFLA has supported hundreds of relatively small teenage pregnancy prevention programs over the years (as well as programs providing support for pregnant and parenting teens), its total funding for abstinence-only education—currently at $13 million—has never been large. However, a lasting contribution of the program was the early development under its auspices of so-called fear-based sex education curricula that use scare tactics about such things as STIs and the failure rates of condoms and have become models for abstinence-only programs nationwide. The "real" money for abstinence-only programs came after 1996, the year in which social conservatives in Congress quietly inserted authorization for a new program into massive legislation designed to overhaul the nation's welfare system. Title V of the Social Security Act includes an ongoing guarantee of $50 million annually to the states; because states must spend $3 for every $4 they receive, the total amount spent pursuant to this program became almost $90 million annually overnight. To qualify for funding, abstinence-only programs must adhere to the requirements of a rigid eight-point definition, including barring teachers from discussing contraceptive methods or safer-sex practices, other than to emphasize their shortcomings, and requiring them to teach that "sexual activity outside of the context of marriage is likely to have harmful psychological and physical effects."

The Evidence Against Abstinence Education

From this considerable base, federal funding for abstinence-only programs accelerated under the Bush administration, especially since the creation in 2000 of a third funding stream also tied to the eight-point definition, the Community-Based Abstinence Education (CBAE) program. Yet, even as funding increased, so did evidence that the approach is ineffective. Ironically, early emanations came in a report issued in 1996, the same year Congress created the Title V abstinence program. An often underemphasized fact about the earlier AFLA program is that it technically is a "demonstration" effort, mandated to test and evaluate various program interventions. The report, conducted by a team of university researchers and entitled *Federally Funded Adolescent Abstinence Promotion Programs: An Evaluation of Evaluations*, concluded that "the quality of the AFLA evaluations funded by the federal government vary from barely adequate to completely inadequate." Moreover, the researchers said, they were aware of "no methodologically sound studies that demonstrate the effectiveness" of abstinence-only curricula.

Over the next decade, however, several well-designed studies began to suggest just how difficult it can be for people to practice abstinence consistently over time. Notable among these is a series of studies examining the effectiveness of virginity pledges, which are the centerpiece of many abstinence education programs. The most recent study, published in the January 2009 issue of *Pediatrics*, found that teens who take virginity pledges are just as likely to have sex as those who do not, but they are less likely to use condoms or other forms of contraception when they become sexually active. This study builds on past research showing that although virginity pledges may help some teens to delay sexual activity, teens who break their pledge are less likely to use contraceptives, are less likely to get tested for STIs and may have STIs for longer periods of time than teens who do not pledge.

A major bombshell dropped two years earlier, however, when a systematic look at the federal abstinence-only effort concluded in 2007 that none of the programs it evaluated were effective in stopping or even delaying sex. The study, mandated by Congress and conducted by Mathematica Policy Research over nine years at a cost of almost $8 million, was initially criticized because it did not look at a nationally representative sample of abstinence-only programs. Instead, it closely examined four programs considered by state officials and abstinence education experts to be especially promising. Even so, after following more than 2,000 teens for as long as six years, the evaluation found that none of the four programs was able to demonstrate a statistically significant beneficial impact on young people's sexual behavior. Individuals who participated in the programs were no more likely to abstain than those who did not.

The Mathematica findings were in keeping with those of another comprehensive review of sex and HIV education programs published later that year. Conducted by Douglas Kirby for the nonpartisan National Campaign to Prevent Teen and Unplanned Pregnancy, *Emerging Answers 2007* concludes that despite improvements in the quality and quantity of evaluation research in this field, "there does not exist any strong evidence that any abstinence program delays the initiation of sex, hastens the return to abstinence, or reduces the number of sexual partners."

Inaccurate Medical Information

On top of this, abstinence-only programs have been sharply criticized by leading medical professional organizations for being, by their very nature, antithetical to the principles of science and medical ethics. As a matter of law, abstinence-only programs are required to promote ideas that are at best scientifically questionable and to withhold health- and life-saving information; as such, they may not credibly assert that they are "medically accurate." Little wonder, then, that leading health professional groups—including the American Medical Association, the American Academy of Pediatrics, the Society for Adolescent Medicine, and the American Psychological Asso-

Nationwide Trend: Rejection of Abstinence Funding

Twenty-three states and the District of Columbia are no longer accepting funds under the Title V abstinence-only education program.

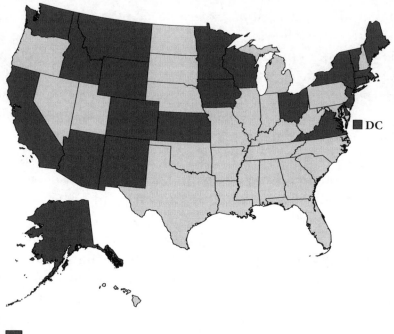

■DC

■ Not accepting funds

Taken From: Heather D. Boonstra, "Advocates Call for a New Approach After Era of 'Abstinence-Only' Education," *Guttmacher Policy Review*, Winter 2009.

ciation—have raised serious ethical concerns about U.S. support for such programs. "Governments have an obligation to provide accurate information to their citizens and to eschew the provision of misinformation in government-funded health education and health care services," says the American Public Health Association in its policy statement on abstinence-only education. "While good patient care is built upon notions of informed consent and free choice, [abstinence-only education] programs are inherently coercive by withholding information needed to make informed choices."

A Common Sense Approach Is Needed

As the evidence base against abstinence-only programs grew, so did the number of states that decided to opt out of the Title V program. To date, 23 states and the District of Columbia have declined to apply for the annual abstinence education grants set aside for them under Title V. The number of adolescents living in those states is substantial: Nearly 14 million young people aged 12–18—46% of those nationwide—reside in states that have passed up abstinence-only funding.

In 2007, policymakers on Capital Hill at long last signaled that, at the very least, the era of big increases for abstinence-only education was over. After many years of expansion, Congress rejected the Bush administration's recommendation to increase funding for CBAE by $28 million and instead kept its funding for FY [fiscal year] 2008 unchanged at $176 million. But the major reversal of political fortune for abstinence-only education came with the 2008 election cycle. President Obama entered the White House with a strong record of support for what he calls "common sense approaches" to preventing unintended pregnancy and HIV, namely "comprehensive sex education that teaches both abstinence and safe sex methods."

Advocates for more comprehensive sex education are now looking to the president and Congress, whose leadership in both houses is dominated by social progressives, to make a more significant break from the past. In light of the wealth of evidence that abstinence-only programs have no beneficial effect on young people's sexual behavior, they are calling on policymakers to stop funding abstinence-only programs altogether and, going further, to create a new funding stream to support programs that are more comprehensive in scope.

Focusing on more comprehensive approaches is both good policy and good politics. It is good policy because it is based on scientific considerations and takes into account the reality of teens' lives. In sharp contrast to abstinence-only programs, there is strong evidence that more comprehensive approaches do help young people both to withstand the pressures to have sex too soon and to have healthy, responsible and mutually protective relationships when they do become sexually active. According to Kirby in *Emerging Answers 2007*, "two-thirds of the 48 comprehensive programs that supported both abstinence and the use of condoms and contraceptives for sexually active teens had positive behavioral effects." Many either delayed or reduced sexual activity, reduced the number of sexual partners or increased condom or contraceptive use. "What is particularly encouraging," said Kirby in a 2007 interview, "is that when some curricula that were found to be effective in one study were implemented by other educators in other states and evaluated by independent research teams, they remained effective if they were implemented with fidelity in the same type of setting and with similar youth."

A New Direction Is Needed

Changing course is also good politics, because it is in sync with what Americans say they want for their children. According to the results of a 2005–2006 nationally representative survey of U.S. adults, published in the *Archives of Pediatrics and Adolescent Medicine*, there is far greater support for comprehensive sex education than for the abstinence-only approach, regardless of respondents' political leanings and frequency of attendance at religious services. Overall, 82% of those polled supported a comprehensive approach, and 68% favored instruction on how to use a condom; only 36% supported abstinence-only education.

As a practical matter, advocates for comprehensive approaches are looking to the Responsible Education About Life (REAL) Act as a model for federal sex education policy in the future.

Introduced in slightly different forms in past years and re-introduced in 2009 in the House and Senate respectively by Rep. Barbara Lee (D-CA) and Sen. Frank Lautenberg (D-NJ), the REAL Act sets out a broad alternative vision for how U.S. policy might best meet the needs of young people. As currently drafted, the bill would authorize at least $50 million annually for five years to support state programs that operate under an eight-point definition of "responsible education," which stands in sharp contrast to the eight-point definition used for the federal abstinence-only funds. Similar to the abstinence-only approach, however, REAL provides a set of principles to guide the content of programs, but leaves curriculum development to local communities.

Of course, passage of the REAL Act is just one step in the larger campaign to support comprehensive sex education. Because sex education programs are guided by policies at multiple levels, from school board policies to city health department regulations to national and state-level laws, policies at each level need to support more comprehensive approaches. And because the REAL Act would direct its funds to state governments, questions remain about funding for community-based organizations and whether some states will decline to apply for the annual comprehensive sex education grants—as many have done under the Title V abstinence program. Moreover, policies and funding must be accompanied by efforts to address a host of other needs, including teacher training, model programs, community assessment tools and program evaluation. Nonetheless, the leadership of the federal government in making sure that young people have the information and skills they will need to make healthy choices about sexual behavior—as teens now and as tomorrow's adults—is critical. In this respect, there is widespread agreement that improvement is both possible and imperative.

| "My faith and the teachings of my church influence my decisions and help me decide with whom I want to spend my time."

Faith-Based Sexual Education Reduces Teen Pregnancy and Provides Needed Guidance

Linda Bales Todd

Linda Bales Todd directs the Louise & Hugh Moore Population Project, an advocacy program focusing on women's issues. In the following viewpoint, Todd states that young people's actions and behavior are strongly influenced by their religious faith. As such, religious institutions have a responsibility to address issues surrounding sexuality among their adolescent populations. Todd cites several studies that found a significantly lower rate of sexual activity and teen pregnancy among young people involved in faith-based institutions, and she notes that many adolescents want their religious organizations to help them reconcile their faith with decisions about sexuality, marriage, and parenting.

As you read, consider the following questions:

1. What percentage of teens taking the Faith Matters survey said their faith is very important or important to them?

2. Why do a large number of religious teens who become pregnant choose to end their pregnancies with abortions, even when they belong to denominations that are strongly pro-life?

3. What did teens in the Faith Matters survey unanimously say they wanted their faith-based institutions to help them with?

Young people's beliefs and behaviors are influenced deeply by their connection with a religious faith as well as their family and peers. The April 2009 *Sex and the Church* article, "Talking to Young People," written by the Rev. Michael Ratliff and James Ritchie, discussed the importance of comprehensive sexuality education. They addressed how the church has and has not responded over the decades to ensure sexuality education is available to young people.

This article includes comments from young people and from a study, "Faith Matters: Teenagers, Religion & Sexuality." The study surveyed teens from Protestant, Roman Catholic, Unitarian Universalist, Jewish and Islamic traditions. Thirty-eight Protestant denominations were represented. The Rev. Steve Clapp, Kristen Leverton Helbert and Angela Zizak Christian Community Inc. in Fort Wayne, Ind., also surveyed 2,049 clergy and 442 adult youth workers.

If the church is to be relevant to young people, we need to listen to their voices and take them seriously on matters related to human sexuality. To do otherwise would cheat the entire denomination [United Methodist] of the wisdom, insight and deeply held religious beliefs they have to offer.

Young People Need Education About Sexuality

Young people who agreed to be interviewed for this article were promised anonymity in regard to their remarks.

"I think young people need more open, frank and honest education about sexuality," said a 25-year-old United Methodist woman. "Young men and women should learn about the changes they are going through and feel that someone is there to answer their questions without judgment."

Her statements are indicative of innumerable other young people who yearn to have a safe place to discuss sexuality.

"My faith and the teachings of my church influence my decisions and help me decide with whom I want to spend my time," this young woman stated. "The most important way [my church] has influenced me is by helping me develop a mature, spiritual understanding of relationships and high expectations for relationships."

How do religious faith and congregational involvement influence the sexual values and behaviors of teenagers? Faith Matters surveyed 5,819 U.S. teenagers involved in faith-based institutions.

- 94% of teen respondents said their faith is very important or important to them. They are very involved in congregational life and place a high priority on congregational activities.

- 71% of teens participate in two or more religious activities each week, in addition to attending worship services.

- Virtually all the teens said they are involved in some religious activity in addition to worship attendance.

- Only 1% percent of teens answered that their faith is not important at all.

Sexual Intercourse and Religion

The United Methodist Church's Social Principles state that sexual relations are only affirmed in the bonds of marriage. We know teens and young adults are having sexual intercourse outside the bonds of marriage, though. The U.S. Centers for Disease Control and Prevention reports that 60.5% of 12th graders across the country have had sexual intercourse.

One 26-year-old talked with me about his unmarried peers having sex. "It doesn't bother me," he said. "Some of my peers are either reckless about sex or in meaningful relationships. If you're safe about it, I'm not too concerned."

He emphasized that safety is the one issue. "Moralizing with peers is not helpful," he shared.

Faith Matters found that teens involved in faith-based institutions show rates of sexual intercourse significantly below those shown in secular studies. Data from Faith Matters show only 31% of 12th graders who are highly involved in congregational life have had sexual intercourse.

The study also discusses a subgroup with deep personal faith and especially involved in church. Among this subgroup 12th graders who have had intercourse drops to 16.5%.

"The general belief is that sex before marriage is not appropriate," said a United Methodist young woman. "The strong proponent of this belief is the church. Little is said or done, though, to help young people deal with these issues."

Other Behaviors and Cultural Practices

Faith Matters study found that many religious teens are involved in other sexual behaviors, including oral sex. Twenty-nine percent of males and 26% of females in the 11th and 12th grades say they have had oral sex.

An alarming response is that 55% of teens surveyed think they cannot contract HIV or another sexually transmitted disease from oral sex.

The study also found that among 11th and 12th grade congregationally involved teens:

- 70% have fondled a partner's breasts and/or genitals.

- Half have been nude with a member of the opposite sex.

- 89% percent of males and 71% of females masturbate.

- Almost all have kissed a member of the opposite sex.

As a global denomination, The United Methodist Church has many diverse cultures involved when discussing sexuality. In many countries experiencing high HIV and AIDS rates, women report that saying "no" to sex is not permissible. Some areas perpetuate the myth that having sex with a virgin will cure a person of AIDS.

In other cultures it's acceptable to stone a woman to death if she has dishonored her family, or to subject her to genital mutilation so that she can't dishonor her family. And, of course, raping women as a spoil and retaliation of war is rampant in some countries.

It's even common in some cultures to "dispose of" female infants. They are considered unwelcome burdens on already-burdened families.

These myths and cultural practices underscore the vital importance of imparting scientifically accurate information to young people.

"Peer groups are key," a young adult told me. "Education is too."

This young adult emphasized that sexuality is a very personal decision. "Every person has to decide for him or herself," he said. "People are wired differently."

Pregnancy and Abortion

"When I got pregnant, my minister was so kind and helpful to me," said a teenager. "I'll never forget how he got my parents to stop being angry."

This young woman expressed some resentment at the church about her situation, though. She asked where the church was before she got pregnant.

"If I'd understood the way my faith should shape my decisions," she said, "I don't think I would have had intercourse."

She also wanted to know why the church or someone failed to teach her about pills or condoms. "I know what I did is my responsibility," she conceded, "but the right information could have changed my life."

Faith Matters found that youths from congregations that provided information about contraception, HIV and other sexually transmitted diseases reported no instances of pregnancy or sexually transmitted disease. This was about 8% of responding congregations. Youths from those congregations were not any more or less likely to have had sexual intercourse.

On the other hand, youths from congregations that did not supply such information were not so fortunate.

- 11% of females who have had intercourse have had a pregnancy.

- 9% of youths who have had intercourse or oral sex have had a sexually transmitted disease.

Half of the teens who became pregnant chose to end that pregnancy with abortion. This included teens from denominational traditions that are strongly pro-life. In many instances, they said that potential disapproval of their families and congregations if they became unwed mothers played a role in the decision to have an abortion.

Unwanted Experiences

I should emphasize that involvement in a faith-based institution does not by and of itself protect teens against unwanted sexual experiences.

Religious Leaders Can Impact Teen Pregnancy Rates

Adults and teens agree that religious leaders and groups should do more to help reduce pregnancy rates among teens.

Teens (Ages 12–19)

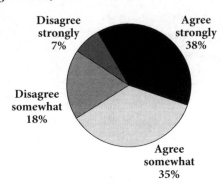

Agree net 73%
Disagree net 24%

Adults

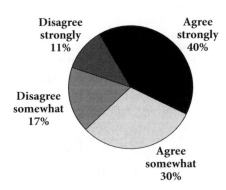

Agree net 70%
Disagree net 28%

Taken From: Bill Albert, *With One Voice 2010: America's Adults and Teens Sound Off About Teen Pregnancy*, The National Campaign to Prevent Teen and Unplanned Pregnancy, December, 2010.

- 31% of the 11th and 12th grade females said they have had an unwanted experience. Force played a role, particularly in those instances where the unwanted experience was intercourse. Social and emotional pressure and poor communication were greater factors, though.

- 90% of female teenagers said they would like programs from their faith-based institutions that would help them develop healthy assertiveness to avoid rape, sexual harassment and abuse.

How the Church Can Respond

Teen participants in the Faith Matters survey gave their congregations poor grades in providing information about sexuality and guidance to prepare for marriage and parenting. Teens were virtually unanimous in wanting their faith-based institutions to do more to help them relate their faith to dating, sexual decision-making, marriage and parenting.

They claimed to be very open to more help from their congregations. They also claimed to be frustrated with the overall failure of adult society to give needed help.

In his classic book *Body Theology*, James Nelson points out the problems that come when our faith communities are silent about sexuality:

> To the extent that our religious communities are sexually silent, we fail to bring faith's resources of support, guidance, and care to deeply significant aspects of our members' experiences.... Our congregations are losing countless teenagers and young adults, not to mention older persons, because they continue to be silent, timid and negative about sexuality.

"Moralistic attitudes toward sexuality can actually increase the likelihood of pregnancy by discouraging contraception without successfully discouraging sexual intercourse."

A Correlation Exists Between Religious Faith and Teen Pregnancy Rates

Joseph M. Strayhorn and Jillian Strayhorn

Joseph M. Strayhorn is affiliated with the Department of Psychiatry at the Drexel University College of Medicine. Jillian Strayhorn is affiliated with the University of Pittsburgh School of Medicine. *The Strayhorns conducted an analysis examining pregnancy rates among teenagers, correlating their findings to the rate of religiosity in the states where the survey participants live. Based on the results, described in this viewpoint, the authors conclude that teens in states with higher religiosity levels show an increased rate of pregnancy compared to teens residing in states with a lower religiosity level. One reason for this corre-*

Joseph M. Strayhorn and Jillian C. Strayhorn, "Religiosity and Teen Birth Rate in the United States," *Reproductive Health*, vol. 6, no. 14, September 17, 2009. Copyright © 2009 by BioMed Central LTD. All rights reserved. Reproduced by permission.

lation, posit the authors, is that teens in religious communities are less likely to use contraception because of their religious beliefs and education; they are not less likely, however, to engage in sexual activity.

As you read, consider the following questions:

1. List three ways in which children of teen mothers have worse outcomes than children born to adult parents, according to the authors.

2. According to the National Public Radio poll cited in the viewpoint, where does the major impetus for abstinence-based education come from? What beliefs form the basis of this point of view?

3. Based on the findings of their study, what conclusion do the authors reach about conservative religious communities and sexual activity among teens that belong to these communities?

The children of teen mothers in the U.S., on the average, have worse outcomes in a number of ways. They score lower in school achievement tests, have a greater likelihood of repeating a grade, are rated more unfavorably by teachers while in high school, have worse physical health, are more likely to be indicated victims of abuse and neglect, have higher durations of foster care placement, and are almost three times more likely to be incarcerated during adolescence or the early 20s than the children of mothers who delayed childbearing; the daughters of teen mothers are more likely to become teen mothers themselves.

In the United States, what to teach adolescents about sexuality and the prevention of teen pregnancy has been controversial. A number of sex education programs in the U.S. have been mandated to be "abstinence-only" programs, excluding the teaching of contraceptive techniques. As stated in a National Public Radio poll report,

> the historical impetus for abstinence education has come from evangelical or born-again Christians. . . . Eighty-one percent of evangelical or born-again Christians believe it is morally wrong for unmarried adults to engage in sexual intercourse, compared with 33 percent of other Americans. . . . More than twice as many evangelicals as non-evangelicals (49 percent to 21 percent) believe the government should fund abstinence-only programs instead of using the money for more comprehensive sex education.

Other polls have presented varying results on similar questions: A 2008 poll in Minnesota reported that a significantly smaller fraction of those who described themselves as "very conservative" politically and those who were "born again" Christian supported comprehensive sex education than the corresponding fractions of more liberal and non-born-again; however, in this sample, 83.2% of the born-again Christians supported comprehensive sex education; only 51% of the politically "very conservative" supported it.

Religiosity and Contraception

The connection between religion and attitudes toward contraception prompts investigation of the relationship between religiosity and teen pregnancy.

Some studies have suggested that greater religiosity is associated with either greater abstinence or lower teen birth rate. [S.A.] Hardy and [M.] Raffaelli, who analyzed data from the National Longitudinal Survey of Youth, reported that higher time one religiosity predicted a lower likelihood of first sexual intercourse between time one and time two. [L.] Loury concluded that communities with larger communities of Catholics and Conservative Protestants have lower rates of teen childbearing, all other things equal. This conclusion was drawn from an analysis of women from age 14–20 in 1979, taken from the National Longitudinal Study of Youth. [D.H.] Mc-Cree and colleagues found that African-American females with higher religiosity scores were more likely to have initiated sex at a later age, to have used a condom in the last six months, and to possess more positive attitudes toward condom use. [S.S.] Rostosky et al. found that adolescent religiosity predicted later coital debut. However, there was a significant interaction between race and religiosity: African-American adolescent males who were either more religious or had signed a virginity pledge were more likely to debut [later] than African-American males who were less religious and/or who had not signed a pledge. [L.] Miller and [M.] Gur found, upon analyzing the National Longitudinal Study of Adolescent Health in the U.S., that frequent attendance of religious events in girls 12 to 21 years old was positively associated with a "responsible and planned use of birth control." Personal conservatism, however, was associated with unprotected sex. [J.] Manlove and colleagues, upon analysis of the 1997 National Longitudinal Survey of Youth, found that in the sample as a whole, greater family religiosity was associated with "using contraceptives consistently"; however, among sexually active males, family religiosity was "directly and negatively associated with contraceptive consistency."

Other studies have suggested that religiosity is associated with behaviors that could lead to a higher teen birth rate. [M.] Studer and [A.] Thornton found that among 18-year-olds, religious teenagers were less likely to use medical methods of contraception when sexually active. [B.] Dodge and colleagues compared male college students in the United States and the Netherlands. American men reported higher rates of inadequate contraception and unwanted pregnancy than their Dutch counterparts; religiosity and sex education were thought to explain these differences.

[J.E.] Rosenbaum compared adolescents who reported taking a virginity pledge with a matched sample of nonpledgers. Among the matching variables was pre-pledge religiosity and attitudes toward sex and birth control. Pledgers did not differ from nonpledgers in lifetime sexual partners and age of first sex, but pledgers were less likely to have used birth control and condoms in the past year and at last sex. This research raises the possibility that moralistic attitudes toward sexuality can actually increase the likelihood of pregnancy by discouraging contraception without successfully discouraging sexual intercourse.

Education About Contraception Helps

Such a hypothesis is bolstered by the research of [J.S.] Santelli and colleagues, who calculated that 86% of the decline in adolescent pregnancies that occurred between 1995 and 2002 was attributable to improved contraceptive use. [J.S.] Santelli and colleagues cite the example of the Netherlands, which in the 1970's went through a period of soul searching and consensus-building about the need for contraception and prevention of sexually transmitted infections in adolescents, and today has one of the lowest teen birth rates in the world. If contraception is more effective than attempted abstinence in reducing birth rates, then attempts to discourage both contraception and sexual intercourse among teenagers could raise teen birth rates.

A complicating variable related to teen births and religiosity is the rate of abortions among teens. [A.] Adamczyk and [J.] Felson, after analyzing longitudinal survey data from the U.S., reported that more highly religious women are less likely to have either an abortion or an out of wedlock pregnancy. [A.] Tomal, upon analyzing data from 1024 counties in 18 U.S. states, found that religious membership level was negatively related to teen abortion rates.

[N.] Cahn and [J.] Carbone summarized differences in attitudes about family and sexuality between the more religious and conservative U.S. "red families," versus the less religious and more liberal "blue families." These authors observed: "Within red families, abstinence outside of marriage is a moral imperative, the shotgun marriage is the preferred solution to an improvident pregnancy, and socialization into traditional gender roles is critical to marital stability." The blue model, however, "involves less control of sexuality, celebrates more egalitarian gender roles, and promotes financial independence and emotional maturity as the sine qua non of responsible parenthood. In this new model, abstinence is unrealistic, contraception is not only permissible, but morally compelled, and abortion is the necessary (and responsible) fallback." Cahn and Carbone mention that teen birth rates appear higher among "red" families.

The present study approaches the relationship between teen birth rate and religiosity by looking at data aggregated across states in the United States. . . .

The Link Between Religiosity and Pregnancy Is Valid

At the state level in the U.S., religiosity, as operationally defined by the eight questions of [a 2008] Pew survey, accurately predicts a high teen birth rate. The significant and high correlation continues to hold after statistically controlling for income and abortion rate.

It is a statistical maxim that higher correlations are to be found using aggregated data, for example state averages, than with individual level data. This is because some of the noise at the individual level is cancelled by the aggregation process, allowing the relationship between signals to be more clear. As stated in an introductory statistics text, "Correlations based on averages are usually too high when applied to individuals." Nonetheless, the magnitude of the correlation between religiosity and teen birth rate astonished us. Teen birth is more highly correlated with some of the religiosity items than some of those items are correlated with each other. We would like to emphasize that we are not attempting to use associations between teen birth rate and religiosity, using data aggregated at the state level, to make inferences at the individual level. It would be a statistical and logical error to infer from our results, "Religious teens get pregnant more often." Such an inference would be an example of the ecological fallacy, which was explicated by [W.S.] Robinson in 1950 and reviewed by [D. A.] Freedman in 2001. The associations we report could still be obtained if, hypothetically, religiosity in communities had an effect of discouraging contraceptive use in the whole community, including the nonreligious teens there, and only the nonreligious teens became pregnant. Or, to create a different imaginary scenario, the results could be obtained if religious parents discouraged contraceptive use in their children, but only nonreligious offspring of such religious parents got pregnant. We create these scenarios simply to illustrate that our ecological correlations do not permit statements about individuals.

We should also caution that on an individual level, certain teen pregnancies are often highly desirable, and some teen parents carry out their responsibilities exceptionally well. If it were possible to obtain good data on unplanned teen pregnancy or pregnancy by "immature" teen parents, we would use it, but we did not find such data available. Nonetheless, at the aggregate level, it is probably true that public policies or cultural practices that reduce the overall rate of teen births are, other things equal, desirable.

Our findings by themselves, of course, do not permit causal inferences. There could be unstudied confounding variables that account for the correlations we report. But if we may speculate on the most probable explanation, drawing on the other research cited above: we conjecture that conservative religious communities in the U.S. are more successful in discouraging use of contraception among their teen community members than in discouraging sexual intercourse itself.

At the level of states in the U.S., conservative religious beliefs predict teen birth rates highly and significantly; the correlation remains high and significant after controlling for income and estimated rates of abortion.

Periodical and Internet Sources Bibliography

The following articles have been selected to supplement the diverse views presented in this chapter.

ABC News	"Abstinence-Only Education Gets a Boost," October 27, 2010. www.abcnews.go.com.
American Life League	"Sex Education: A Parent's Right, A Parent's Responsibility," October 28, 2010. www.ewtn.com.
Emily Holcombe, David Carrier, Jennifer Manlove, and Suzanne Ryan	"Contraceptive Use Patterns Across Teens' Sexual Relationships," *Child Trends*, February, 2008.
Natalie Ingraham	"Does Peer-Led Sex Education Work?" Kinsey Confidential, November 8, 2010. www.kinseyconfidential.com.
Barbara Miner	"We're Here. We're Sexual. Get Used to It," *Colorlines*, June 2008.
Jessie L. Nelson	"Saving the Next Generation; The Black Church's Response to Teen Pregnancy," *African American Pulpit*, April 1, 2010.
Janet Elise Rosenbaum	"Patient Teenagers? A Comparison of the Sexual Behavior of Virginity Pledgers and Matched Nonpledgers," *Pediatrics*, January 2009.
David A. Ross	"Approaches to Sex Education: Peer-Led or Teacher-Led?" *PLoS Medicine*, vol. 5, no. 11, November 2008.
Scotsman.com	"Teenagers to Teach Sex Education," April 11, 2010.

CHAPTER 4

How Should Society Respond to Teenage Sexuality?

Chapter Preface

In 2008, Gloucester High School, in Massachusetts, reported a sudden spike in the number of pregnant students— eighteen by the end of the school year, more than quadruple the number of pregnancies from the previous year. The story made national headlines when some news sources reported that a group of sixteen girls at Gloucester High made a pact to get pregnant together. The "pregnancy pact" was never confirmed, but the story set off a firestorm of debate about related issues, one of which was minors' right to confidential reproductive services. In 2008, based on the high number of students who sought pregnancy tests and related services between 2007 and 2008, Gloucester High's student clinic began advocating for permission to provide contraceptives to student clients without parental consent or notification. In the aftermath of the "pregnancy pact" story, the push for confidential reproductive services for adolescents took center stage in Gloucester, with strong supporters for and against the idea. In October 2008, Gloucester schools approved the dissemination of contraceptives through their school clinic, based on prior parent approval.

The availability of confidential reproductive services to minors has a long, involved history in the United States. Although public opinion reveals a consistent resistance to the notion of minors' ability to seek confidential medical care, the Public Health Service Act of 1970, better known as Title X, guarantees provision of confidential health services to people, regardless of age. This includes the ability of minors to get contraceptives. Although the intent of the original bill was to encourage parent involvement in such decisions, school clinics are not required to inform parents if their children seek reproductive services. Legislative efforts by conservatives, first in 1982 and then again in 1990, to change the law have been largely unsuccessful. Both times regulation that would have required Title X–funded clinics to notify parents before dispensing contraceptives to minors was defeated. Since then, the Patient Protection and Affordable Care Act (PPACA) of 2010, the health care reform legislation supported by President Barack Obama, extended and solidified legal, confidential access to reproductive health services for minors. The decision was supported by many, including the American Academy of Pediatrics, the American Academy of Family Physicians, and the American College of Obstetricians and Gynecologists.

As of 2010, no state explicitly requires parental consent or notification for contraceptive services except Utah and Texas, where parental consent is needed for contraceptive services when a clinic uses state funds. Advocates of minors' right to privacy note that the guarantee of confidentiality, especially regarding reproductive services, is a key component in encouraging minors to access and use contraceptives. While parental consent is desirable, the Guttmacher Institute notes that, in reality, many sexually active minors would avoid using contraceptives if doing so necessitated obtaining parental consent. The result, notes Guttmacher, would be increasing numbers of unwanted pregnancies and a spread of STDs.

Opponents of minors' access to confidential reproductive services have so far lost the legal battle but continue to advocate a reconsideration of the law. They believe legalizing minors' rights to confidential reproductive services, including the ability to prescribe contraceptives to students, encourages teens to engage in early sexual activity. Instead, they argue that sex education programs should implement efforts to inform and include parents in their minors' decisions about health care, noting that parental disapproval is a strong deterrent to early sexual activity.

According to this point of view, teen pregnancy is a larger social and cultural problem, one that cannot be fully addressed by providing greater access to confidential birth control. Daniel Patrick Moloney of The Heritage Foundation notes, referring to sexually active teens: "It's difficult to imagine a more counterproductive approach. These girls need more parental involvement, not less. These young girls *know how* to have babies, so further sex ed isn't needed. They *want* to have babies, so contraception is beside the point. The problem is that they think they *are ready* to have babies, and they aren't."

Since minors can, by law, seek confidential reproductive services, many who continue to oppose the guidelines have been utilizing statutory rape laws in order to get around the issue. Although these laws vary by state, the requirement to report underage sexual activity is sometimes used by clinics to include parents in minors' health decisions about contraceptives.

Legislating issues pertaining to minors, especially related to teen sexuality, is a difficult and complex process, with strong opinions expressed on all sides of on any given issue. The viewpoints in the chapter that follows illustrate this difficulty by discussing other legal issues related to teenage sexuality.

> *"Given that so many students will not abstain from sex, programs have an obligation to help teens understand the risks and responsibilities that come with sexual activity."*

Government Should Support and Fund Comprehensive Sex Education

National Partnership for Women & Families

The National Partnership for Women & Families is a nonprofit organization whose goal is to promote fairness in the workplace, reproductive health and rights, and access to affordable health care for all sections of the population. The following viewpoint was submitted to the House Committee on Oversight and Government Reform and argues for continued funding of comprehensive sex education. According to the authors, although abstinence from sexual activity is a worthy goal, programs that stress abstinence over comprehensive sex education are ineffective at delaying sexual initiation and do not deserve the level of government funding allocated to them. Instead, given the support for comprehensive sex education among parents, funding from government-sponsored sex education programs should be applied to such broad programs, helping to cover important gaps in today's sex education curricula.

As you read, consider the following questions:

1. What are two major misconceptions about contraceptives held by many teens, as explained in this viewpoint?

2. Why are current federal abstinence guidelines ethically problematic, according to the authors of this viewpoint?

3. List three positive outcomes for teens who participated in comprehensive sex education programs.

The National Partnership for Women & Families is pleased to submit a statement for today's [April 23, 2008] hearing in the House Committee on Oversight and Government Reform, "Domestic Abstinence-Only Programs: Assessing the Evidence." Our statement highlights a few of the reasons—practical, public health, and ethical—to question continuing the public investment in ideologically driven abstinence-only-until-marriage programs. These programs promote abstinence from sexual activity, often providing incomplete and/or misleading information about contraception and sexually transmitted infections (STIs). They also prescribe unrealistic, marriage-focused goals that run counter to the life choices of virtually all Americans.

Certainly, the National Partnership recognizes that abstinence, especially for young teens, is the healthiest choice. We strongly support encouraging teens to postpone sexual activity, and we know that parents, health care providers, and other responsible adults have critical roles to play in instilling values and educating children and teens about sexual development and responsible behavior and decision-making.

Comprehensive Sex Education Funding Is Needed

At the same time, it is critical that Congress acknowledge the growing body of evidence that confirms that abstinence-only programs are not effective at delaying sexual initiation, preventing unwanted pregnancy, or reducing STIs. Federal and state governments have invested more than $1.3 billion in these programs since 1997 and evidence shows that they are at best, ineffective, and at worst, dangerous to America's youth. Programs that refuse or fail to teach our youth how to protect themselves against unwanted pregnancy and sexually transmitted infections leave them more vulnerable to unintended pregnancy, HIV/AIDS and other diseases. In addition, abstinence-only programs also offer little to teens who are already sexually active, encourage further stigmatization of those who may be gay, lesbian, bisexual, or transgender, and put health educators in the untenable and unethical position of having to withhold vital information. . . .

Parents Favor Comprehensive Sex Education

The vast majority of parents favor sex education that is comprehensive, medically accurate, and age-appropriate—with good reason. Parents see such courses and content as supplementing, not supplanting, their discussions at home. They want their children to be taught the benefits of delaying the onset of intimate sexual relationships until they are mature and responsible *and* to be given the information and skills they need to use condoms and contraception when they choose to become sexually active.

According to a poll conducted in 2003 by the Kaiser Family Foundation, National Public Radio, and Harvard University, only 15 percent of Americans believe that schools should only teach abstinence from sexual intercourse and should not provide information on condoms and other contraception. A

March 2007 poll of registered voters conducted by the National Women's Law Center and Planned Parenthood Federation of America yielded similar results, with more than three out of four respondents preferring comprehensive sex education curricula, while only 14 percent supported teaching "abstinence only" in public schools.

Most parents believe that teens are capable of absorbing a two-pronged message: abstinence from sexual activity is best until you are in a committed, loving relationship, but if and when you engage in sexual activity, be responsible and know how to protect yourself and your partner. . . .

Government-Sponsored Programs Should Fill the Information Gap

Given that so many students will not abstain from sex, programs have an obligation to help teens understand the risks and responsibilities that come with sexual activity. Survey after survey indicates that adolescents have a tremendous unmet need for information related to sexuality, contraception, STIs, and making sexual decisions.

A nationwide survey conducted by the Kaiser Family Foundation and *Seventeen Magazine* found considerable gaps in teens' knowledge. The survey found that many teens hold misconceptions and harbor unnecessary and unfounded fears—such as the belief that contraception can cause infertility or birth defects. Nearly 20 percent of surveyed teens underestimated the effectiveness of the contraceptive patch or ring, and more than 25 percent said they believed that emergency contraception causes abortion. Few teens understood the effectiveness of the male condom in preventing STIs, including HIV. In addition, more than 25 percent of the teens did not know that oral contraception provides no protection against sexually transmitted diseases.

The government-sponsored abstinence evaluation conducted by Mathematica Policy Research confirmed that teens

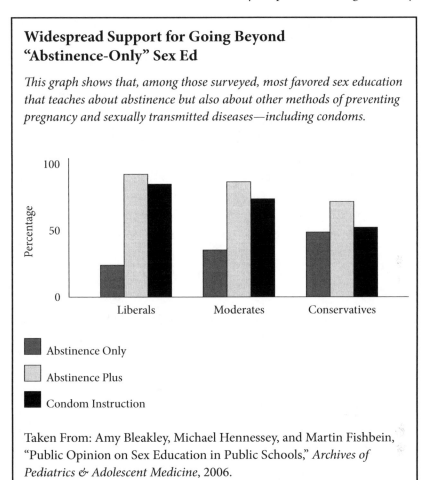

Widespread Support for Going Beyond "Abstinence-Only" Sex Ed

This graph shows that, among those surveyed, most favored sex education that teaches about abstinence but also about other methods of preventing pregnancy and sexually transmitted diseases—including condoms.

Taken From: Amy Bleakley, Michael Hennessey, and Martin Fishbein, "Public Opinion on Sex Education in Public Schools," *Archives of Pediatrics & Adolescent Medicine*, 2006.

have important gaps in knowledge of STIs. The study found that on average, youth got only about half the answers correct regarding the health consequences of STIs.

The March 2008 CDC [Centers for Disease Control and Prevention] data on sexually transmitted infections reinforces the need for medically accurate information and greater utilization of health service.

CDC's data on sexually transmitted infections is a sobering reminder that teenage girls need better information, as well as more screening and treatment. The fact that at least one in four teenage girls nationwide—more than three million teens—has a sexually transmitted infection is a measure of our failure. We should be taking money from the abstinence-only programs that don't work, and instead putting it into sexuality and prevention programs that will reduce these appalling numbers.

Given that the health effects of STIs for women—from infertility to cervical cancer—are particularly severe, there is no time to waste. STI screening, vaccination and other prevention strategies for sexually active women should be among our highest public health priorities, especially since an estimated half of all new HIV infections occur in people under age 25.

For Health Care Providers, Withholding Information Is Unethical

Health care providers and health educators have ethical obligations to provide accurate health information. Patients and students have a right to the most accurate and complete information—information that can help young people achieve good health outcomes. Current federal abstinence laws and guidelines are ethically problematic because they limit the information—including accurate information about contraception and safer sex—available to young people. So it is not surprising that many highly respected national organizations support comprehensive sex education, including the American Academy of Pediatrics, American College of Obstetricians and Gynecologists, American Medical Association, American Public Health Association, National Campaign to Prevent Teen Pregnancy, National Education Association, National Medical Association, National School Boards Association, and the Society for Adolescent Medicine, among many others. . . .

Funding Abstinence Programs Wastes Money

The $1.3 billion in federal and state expenditures for abstinence-only programs is money poorly spent.

The claims made by abstinence-only proponents—that comprehensive sexuality education promotes promiscuity, hastens the initiation of sex or increases its frequency, and sends a confusing message to adolescents—are specious. A congressionally-mandated study conducted for the Department of Health and Human Services by Mathematic Policy Research and released last year reviewed four separate abstinence programs. Youth in the four programs were no more likely than other youth to have abstained from sex in the four to six years after they began participating in the study. Youth in both groups who reported having sex had similar numbers of sexual partners and had initiated sex at the same average age.

A review of federally funded programs by researcher Doug Kirby released in November of 2007 found that programs that focused exclusively on abstinence did not affect teen sexual behavior. The report found that, "At present there does not exist any strong evidence that any abstinence program delays the initiation of sex, hastens the return to abstinence or reduces the number of sexual partners" among teenagers. The study found that while abstinence-only efforts appear to have little positive impact, more comprehensive sex education programs were having "positive outcomes" including teenagers "delaying the initiation of sex, reducing the frequency of sex, reducing the number of sexual partners and increasing condom or contraceptive use." "Two-thirds of the 48 comprehensive programs that supported both abstinence and the use of condoms and contraceptives for sexually active teens had positive behavior effect," the report found. Such programs improved teens' knowledge about the risks and consequences of pregnancy and sexually transmitted diseases, and gave them greater "confidence in their ability to say 'no' to unwanted sex."

Just this month [April 2008], a report in the *Journal of Adolescent Health* concluded that abstinence-only programs have "no significant effect" on "delaying the initiation of sexual activity or in reducing the risk for teen pregnancy" and STIs. Authors added that comprehensive sexuality education programs significantly reduced the risk of pregnancy when compared with abstinence-only education or no sexuality education at all. Comprehensive sex education also was associated with a marginally reduced likelihood of a teen becoming sexually active, when compared with no sex education. Researchers note that, because their findings indicated a decreased likelihood of pregnancy among teens who received comprehensive sex education, adolescents who received abstinence-only education might "engage in higher risk behaviors once they initiate sexual activity." Although further research is needed to examine the effects of formal sex education, the study's findings "suggest that formal comprehensive sex education programs reduce the risk for teen pregnancy without increasing the likelihood that adolescents will engage in sexual activity," and these findings "confirm results from randomized controlled trials that abstinence-only programs have minimal effect on sexual risk behavior."

An earlier report issued in December of 2004 by the Minority Staff of the House Committee on [Oversight and] Government Reform found that more than two-thirds of abstinence-programs funded under Title V are using curricula with multiple scientific and medical inaccuracies. These curricula contained misinformation about condoms, abortion, and basic scientific facts, such as:

- "tears" and "sweat" can transmit HIV;

- condoms do not help prevent the spread of STDs;

- 5% to 10% of women who have legal abortions will become sterile;

- a 43-day-old fetus is a "thinking person."

Many also blurred religion and science and presented gender stereotypes as fact.

Many states and well-regarded researchers have conducted evaluations and arrived at similar conclusions. Scott Frank of Case Western Reserve University School of Medicine in Cleveland found that the curricula used in Ohio's abstinence-only programs—offered in 85 out of 88 counties—contained false and misleading information about abortion and contraception. It also found that the curricula reinforced gender stereotypes and notions about sex that are not based in science. One program told teens they should "be prepared to die" if they use condoms because they are likely to fall off or break, according to Frank's study.

States Are Turning Down Funding

The most compelling verdict on the program comes from the states—17 of which have turned down Title V abstinence funds even in the face of economic downturns that have left them scrambling for resources. Many have based their decisions on the growing number of state and national evaluations that call into question the efficacy and accuracy of abstinence-only programs.

It is past time for the federal government to stop funding ideologically-based abstinence-only programs that are failing our young people, and instead use those resources to fund comprehensive sexuality education programs that will help reduce unintended pregnancy, reduce the spread of sexually transmitted infections including HIV/AIDS, and help young people make responsible choices.

"The majority of parents surveyed favor their adolescents receiving abstinence messages from multiple sources."

Government Should Support and Fund Abstinence Education

Eric Young

Eric Young is a reporter for the Christian Post. *In the following viewpoint, Young discusses the results of a study that reveals attitudes and opinions among parents and adolescents about sex and abstinence messages. According to Young, parents prefer that adolescents receive abstinence messages from a variety of sources, including schools and community organizations. The study cited by Young concluded that abstinence messages taught in school sex education programs resulted in increased levels of communication about sex and abstinence among families and peers. Government funding of sex education should reflect the values of most parents and teens, a majority of whom support abstinence education in schools.*

As you read, consider the following questions:

1. In order of preference, what are the major sources cited by parents from which their adolescents should receive abstinence messages?

2. What is one major concern expressed by Valerie Huber, as cited in this viewpoint, regarding sex education policy being implemented by the Obama administration?

3. According to this viewpoint, how has increased lobbying against abstinence programs affected teen pregnancy?

After having stonewalled public requests for months, the [Barack] Obama administration relented this past week [in August 2010] in releasing a taxpayer-supported study on the attitudes and opinions of adolescents and their parents regarding sex, abstinence, and abstinence messages.

The 2009 study, titled the "National Survey of Adolescents and Their Parents: Attitudes and Opinions about Sex and Abstinence," was prepared by Cambridge, Mass.–based Abt Associates for the Family and Youth Services Bureau, the Administration for Children and Families, and the U.S. Department of Health and Human Services.

Findings Reveal Parents Support Abstinence Education

It revealed, among other pro-abstinence findings, that the majority of parents surveyed favor their adolescents receiving abstinence messages from multiple sources. Ordered from most preferred to least preferred, parents favored abstinence messages delivered at a place of worship (85 percent), a doctor's office or health center (85 percent), school (83 percent), a community organization (71 percent), and the internet (55 percent).

The study also examined where adolescents were exposed to information about sex and abstinence.

According to the study, adolescents largely learned in school how to resist pressures to have sexual intercourse, with 93 percent saying that is where they were exposed to the information. Only 34 percent said they were exposed to the information in a place of worship; 21 percent from a doctor's office, health center or health care clinic; 11 percent from a community organization; and 7 percent from some other place.

As for how babies are made, pregnancy or birth, 97 percent of adolescents said they learned in school; 31 percent in a place of worship; 24 percent from a doctor's office, health center or health care clinic: 13 percent from a community organization; and 6 percent from some other place.

And when it came to the abstinence message—waiting until marriage to have sexual intercourse—80 percent of adolescents said they were exposed in school; 53 percent in a place of worship; 18 percent from a doctor's office, health center or health care clinic; 11 percent from a community organization; and 8 percent from some other place.

Notably, however, 68.3 percent of adolescents identified a family member as the preferred source of information about sex and sexual issues, with mothers being the most favored source (43.9 percent). Only 8.7 percent said a teacher was the preferred source—the fourth most popular after friends (17.4 percent) and fathers (13.7 percent).

"In general, our findings indicate that adolescent attitudes about sex and abstinence are more subject to influence from parents and peers than to messages about sex and abstinence delivered in the context of classes or programs," the authors of the study concluded. "However, adolescent receipt of information about sex, abstinence, and sexual values in a class or program was associated with increased levels of adolescent communication about sex and abstinence with both parents and peers."

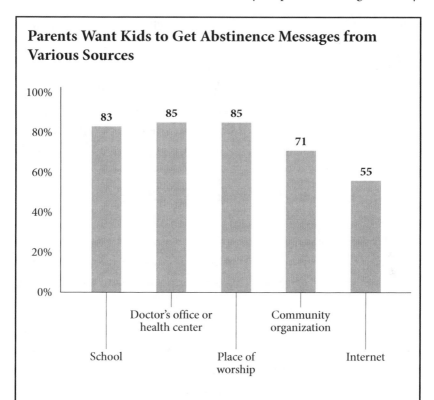

Parents Want Kids to Get Abstinence Messages from Various Sources

Taken From: "National Survey of Adolescents And Their Parents: Attitudes And Opinions about Sex and Abstinence," Family and Youth Services Bureau, US Department of Health and Human Services, February 26, 2009.

Sex Education Policy Should Reflect America's Values

Following the release of the study, Valerie Huber, executive director of National Abstinence Education Association (NAEA), expressed "great concern" over the sex education policy that is being implemented by the Obama administration, which she said does not reflect the values of what most parents and teens clearly want.

"It is important that the representative government reflects the desires of its constituents," she commented a day after the study's release. "This study's findings call for a reinstatement of funding for abstinence education within the next fiscal budget."

On Sept. 30 [2010], more than 170 abstinence programs will lose funding for their abstinence-centered programs because Congress and the Obama administration canceled all grants going to abstinence-centered programming in their FY2010 budget.

Some programs, NAEA reported, will lose their funding midstream in their five-year grant award.

"This means that nearly two million students will return to school without the skill-building lessons they have come to expect in their abstinence education classes," the organization added.

It was for this and other reasons that the NAEA mobilized grassroots pressure on the Obama administration to release the study after some of its findings were released in conferences last year and in an executive level report that was made available online.

Dr. Lisa Rue, who wanted to see the full study after first hearing about it in a conference, was among those who were denied access after formally requesting it via the Freedom of Information Act (FOIA).

According to Rue, the Obama administration denied her request, citing an FOIA exemption that permits withholding information that is "predecisional" and "deliberative."

But after a second denial months later, Rue sounded off, arguing that enough time had passed for closed-door deliberations to take place.

"It is time for openness and dissemination, which is what we expect from an administration that is advocating change in our society," she expressed in an editorial in the *Times Call*. "It is time to invite the people in to weigh the facts and have a voice in the type of prevention and heath promotion programs offered via school districts and community based organizations."

With help from the NAEA, hundreds submitted FOIA requests earlier this month for public release of the findings.

Abstinence-Only Messages Are Essential

Following the study's release, the NAEA called into question whether recent sex education policy decisions truly reflect cultural norms or clear evidence-based trends.

"Teen-sex advocacy groups have pushed for an end to abstinence education funding, despite the fact that a recent HHS [Health and Human Services] study showed most teens and their parents support the core message of the program," the organization noted.

"If we are truly interested in learning how to prevent two critical epidemics currently devastating our country (out-of-wedlock child bearing and sexually transmitted infections) then the nationally representative findings provide momentum and support for accessing cultural values of parents and children, which promote optimal health choices for adolescents," added Rue.

For nearly two decades, the teen birth rate in the United States has been dropping and according to the latest report by the Centers for Disease Control and Prevention's National Center for Health Statistics, there were 41.5 births per 1,000 teenagers aged 15–19 years in 2008.

Between 2005 and 2006 there was an increase in teen birth rates, which abortion rights groups said coincided with an increase in "rigid abstinence-only-until-marriage programs" that received a boost in funding under the [George W.] Bush administration.

Pro-lifers, however, suggested that there may have been more teen pregnancies because of Planned Parenthood's increased lobbying against abstinence programs. Only when it became popular to teach the abstinence message to teens did the pregnancy rates begin to fall in the early 1990s, contended groups such as American Life League.

Notably, after another increase in 2007, the birth rate for teens aged 15 to 19 dropped to the figure recorded for 2008. Teenagers that year accounted for 22 percent of all non-marital births.

> "*Creating, possessing, or disseminating sexually explicit photographs of a minor, even when self-produced, may violate state and federal child pornography statutes.*"

Teen Sexting Should Be Regulated but Not Considered Child Pornography

Sarah Wastler

Sarah Wastler holds a bachelor's degree from Georgetown University and a law degree from Harvard Law School. In the following viewpoint, Wastler provides legal context for current laws regarding sexting. Wastler specifically addresses the impact of these laws on teenagers and minors and notes that current pornography laws treat minors engaged in sexting in the same manner as adults being prosecuted for pornography. According to Wastler, legal regulation of the sexting phenomenon is needed and necessary, but many questions must be resolved before a wide-ranging legal response to sexting can be put into action.

Sarah Wastler, "The Harm in 'Sexting'?: Analyzing the Constitutionality of Child Pornography Statutes that Prohibit the Voluntary Production, Possession, and Dissemination of Sexually Explicit Images by Teenagers," *Harvard Journal of Law and Gender*, vol. 33, no. 2, 2010, pp. 687–95, 698–99, 701–02. Copyright © 2010. Republished with permission of Harvard University Law School, conveyed through Copyright Clearance Center, Inc.

As you read, consider the following questions:

1. Can minors be charged and found guilty of child pornography?

2. Why does Wastler believe that sexting should be considered outside the scope of child pornography?

3. Give one reason why, according to the author, child pornography should be treated as a new and unique problem in the penal system.

A new trend among teenagers has recently triggered concern among parents and educators and fascinated the media. However, unlike many adolescent fads that provoke dismay from the older generation, "sexting"—the transmission of sexually explicit photos via text message—has resulted in serious consequences for some participants. Creating, possessing, or disseminating sexually explicit photographs of a minor, even when self-produced, may violate state and federal child pornography statutes. Although the statutes prohibiting child pornography (as well as the severe penalties for violation) were enacted to address a very different crime—"the rape and molestation of children, captured on film or in other visual formats"—the laws do not explicitly exempt images that were voluntarily produced and disseminated by the minors themselves. As a result, prosecutors have brought child pornography charges against some "sexters," and others have used the threat of prosecution to encourage cooperation with non-penal actions designed to deter the practice of sexting and to educate minors about its dangers.

Some Sexting Is Deliberate and Voluntary

These cases not only give rise to a contentious debate regarding the appropriate methods of prevention and response to adolescents who voluntarily produce and disseminate sexually explicit images of themselves, but also raise serious questions regarding the constitutionality of prosecuting such juveniles under existing child pornography frameworks. In reality, there is a wide range of circumstances under which minors engage in the production and dissemination of sexually explicit images of themselves that involves varying levels of coercion and consent. Although existing societal mores and social dynamics may undermine a vision of such conduct as an exercise of free choice, this [viewpoint] posits that under some circumstances, these images must be considered voluntary. This [viewpoint] focuses its analysis on a sexting paradigm in which a minor takes explicit photographs of him or herself or records a sexual encounter with the cooperation and consent of any other participants and voluntarily distributes, at least to an initial recipient or recipients, such images.

This [viewpoint] argues that existing child pornography statutes are unconstitutional to the extent that they proscribe the voluntary production and dissemination of self-produced pornographic images. Part I introduces the legal issues raised by sexting prosecutions by examining the facts of the high-profile case, *Miller v. Mitchell*. Part II outlines the scope of permissible First Amendment regulations. Part III discusses the applicability of statutory definitions of child pornography to sexting images in their plain language and purpose. After analyzing the child pornography exception to the First Amendment, Part IV concludes that self-produced sexual images of minors do not satisfy the definition of child pornography so as to warrant inclusion within the category of unprotected speech because such images are not intrinsically related to the sexual abuse of children. This [viewpoint] concludes by proposing potential methods for regulating self-produced pornographic images of minors outside the framework of child pornography and articulates lingering questions that must be addressed before a comprehensive response to the problem of sexting can be implemented.

Part I: Prosecution and the Sexting Phenomenon

Although a serious debate exists over whether it is appropriate to punish teenagers engaged in sexting in the criminal and juvenile justice systems, [Amanda Lenhart writes that] "[s]ome law enforcement officers and district attorneys have begun prosecuting teens who created and shared such images under laws generally reserved for producers and distributors of child pornography." In *Miller v. Mitchell*, the U.S. Court of Appeals for the Third Circuit became the first federal appellate court to address the difficult questions surrounding [what Nathan Gorenstein described as] "sexting, the reach of the state child pornography law, and the First Amendment." The case began in 2008 when school officials in Tukahannock High School discovered saved images of scantily clad, nude, or semi-nude teenage girls on several students' confiscated cell phones. Believing that the male students were trading such images, the school district turned the phones over to the District Attorney of Wyoming County, George Skumanick. The District Attorney's office subsequently notified the parents of twenty students who appeared in or possessed such images that the students would be required to participate in a six to nine month education program or face criminal charges.

Although most of the students implicated eventually agreed to participate in a five week education program to avoid criminal prosecution, Nancy Doe, Grace Kelly and Marissa Miller, and their parents, represented by the American Civil Liberties Union ("ACLU"), filed suit against Skumanick alleging that he had threatened prosecution in retaliation against their exercise of their First Amendment rights to free expression and right to be free from compelled expression, as well as their parents' exercise of their Fourteenth Amendment rights to direct their children's upbringings. Plaintiffs argued that the images did not constitute child pornography and that the girls could not be charged because they did not consent to the distribution of the images that pictured them. Finding that plaintiffs were likely to prevail on the merits, the district court granted a temporary restraining order prohibiting Skumanick from initiating criminal charges against plaintiffs for the two photographs in question.

Judge Ambro of the Third Circuit, writing for a unanimous three-judge panel, affirmed the grant of a preliminary injunction preventing the District Attorney from bringing charges against Nancy Doe. The court held that plaintiffs showed a likelihood of success on their claims—that any prosecution would not be based on probable cause, but instead would be in retaliation in violation of Nancy Doe's exercise of her constitutional right to be free from compelled speech and in violation of Jane Doe's right to direct her child's upbringing. However, the court declined to address the additional claim that any prosecution would be in retaliation in violation of the "minors' First Amendment right to free expression, the expression being their appearing in two photographs." The court also declined to rule on whether "the sexual abuse of children law applies to a minor depicted in the allegedly pornographic photograph" and whether "the photo in question could constitute a 'prohibited sexual act.'" The court, however, was adamant that merely "appearing in a photograph provides no evidence as to whether that person possessed or transmitted the photo."

Although *Miller* is a peculiar case due both to the relatively innocuous nature of the photos in question and an unusual nudity provision in the Pennsylvania child pornography statute, it raised critical questions regarding the constitutionality of prosecuting minors for the production, dissemination, and possession of self-produced sexually explicit images. News articles abound with other examples of teenagers facing criminal charges for sexting and courts will likely have ample opportunity to address the outstanding constitutional questions.

Although the problem of young people photographing themselves is as old as the Polaroid, new mediums create new problems of over-exposure and permanency. Sexted images are frequently forwarded by the original recipient without the consent of the individual pictured in the image. Developing an appropriate response to the issue of sexting will require a serious inquiry into First Amendment doctrine, the purposes of child pornography regulations, and the consequences of conflating the sexual abuse of children with sexting, [described by David Rosen as] "a post-modern form of flirting, a game of sexual show-&-tell."

Part II: The First Amendment and the Limits of Protection

The First Amendment commands that "Congress shall make no law ... abridging the freedom of speech." Despite this emphatic language, the protections of the First Amendment are not absolute. Expression, for example, may be restricted on the basis of time, place, or manner, "provided that such regulations are justified without reference to the content of the regulated speech, that they are narrowly tailored to serve a significant governmental interest, and that they leave open ample alternative channels for communication of the information" [*Clark v. Cmty. for Creative Non-Violence*, 1984]. The First Amendment, however, does generally proscribe efforts by the government to restrict speech or expressive conduct based on the disapproval of the ideas expressed. Content-based regulations, especially those enforced by severe criminal penalties, "have the constant potential to be a repressive force in the lives and thoughts of a free people" [*Ashcroft v. ACLU*, 2004] and are therefore presumptively invalid. When a statute regulates speech on the basis of content, the government bears the burden of proving that the regulation is narrowly tailored to promote a compelling government interest.

Prosecuting Sexting Victimizes the Victims

There's good reason to be concerned about teens being self-pornographers. But many, especially legal experts, are disturbed by the fact that a healthy horn-dog of a teenager could be grouped in the same criminal category as a clinically ill pedophile. . . .

Reed Lee, a Chicago attorney and board member of the Free Speech Coalition, says: "A law to protect victims shouldn't send those very victims to jail."

Tracy Clark-Flory, "The New Pornographers,"
Salon, February 20, 2009. www.salon.com.

The First Amendment prohibits content-based regulations in order to prevent the government from "effectively driv[ing] certain ideas or viewpoints from the marketplace" of ideas [*Davenport v. Washington Education Association*, 2007]. However, the Supreme Court has recognized a few limited categories of speech that do not play an essential role in the expression of ideas and are of such slight value that "any benefit that may be derived from them is clearly outweighed by the social interest in order and morality" [*Chaplinsky v. New Hampshire*, 1942]. Within these narrow classes of material, including obscenity and, more recently, child pornography, the prevention and punishment of speech has never been thought to raise any serious constitutional objections. . . .

Part III: Current Child Pornography Regulations Do Prohibit Sexting

Because "it is impossible to determine whether a statute reaches too far without first knowing what the statute covers"

[*United States v. Williams*, 2008] it is necessary to determine whether the production, dissemination, receipt, and possession of sexually explicit text messages fall within the prohibition under existing child pornography regulations. Although child pornography laws vary across jurisdictions, the statutes typically prohibit the production, dissemination, or possession of sexually explicit images of minors in terms broad enough to reach some self-produced images.

Determining whether self-produced images satisfy definitions of child pornography requires a fact intensive inquiry into the content of specific images in specific cases. Under federal law, for example, it is a crime for "*any* person" to knowingly receive, distribute, or possess any visual depiction the production of which "involve[d] the *use* of a minor engaging in sexually explicit conduct." Similarly, it is a crime for any person to "employ[], *use*[], persuade[], induce[], entice[], or coerce[] any minor to engage in . . . any sexually explicit conduct for the purpose of producing any visual depiction of such conduct. . . ." Sexually explicit conduct, in turn, is defined to include not only several specifically enumerated sexual acts, but also "lascivious exhibition of the genitals or pubic area."

Not all self-produced images contain depictions of sexually explicit conduct, and there is also some question as to whether a minor has been "used" in the production of self-produced images. It seems clear that when the producer of the image is not the pictured individual or when more than one minor engages in and records a sexual act, the production of such images would involve the "use" of a minor. It is less clear, however, that when a minor takes an explicit photograph of him or herself, he or she could be charged with production. Can an individual employ, use, persuade, induce, or entice oneself? There is some argument, at least, that when read in context, "use" seems to contemplate or require another individual involved in the production other than the minor-subject of the images. With no explicit age restrictions such as the "Romeo and Juliet" exceptions found in some statutory rape laws, minors, no less than adults, can be charged and found guilty of child pornography offenses if the sexted image satisfies the legal definition. . . .

Part IV: Sexting Is Not Child Pornography

Recent Supreme Court jurisprudence has defined child pornography as an unprotected category of speech separate from traditional obscenity limitations to the extent that such images are intrinsically related to the crime of child sexual abuse. As previously discussed, content-based regulations are presumptively invalid and the government must show that any regulations that restrict free expression are narrowly tailored to promote a compelling government interest. With regard to a narrow class of well-defined exceptions, the Court has foregone the necessity of case-by-case adjudication, reflecting the calculus that the "evil to be restricted so overwhelmingly outweighs the expressive interests . . . at stake." The "inherent dangers of undertaking to regulate any form of expression" and anxiety over heavy-handed censorship, however, have resulted in the careful tailoring of the scope of these categorical exceptions. . . .

Sexting should be considered outside the scope of the child pornography exclusion because such images, like virtual child pornography, do not involve the sexual abuse of a child. When, as in sexting, the images in question lack a proximate connection to the crime of child rape, the images fall outside the confines of the child pornography category of speech because the government interest in protecting the victims of child sexual abuse is no longer present and cannot justify the wholesale exclusion from First Amendment protection. An adolescent taking nude or scantily clad photos of themselves or recording their consensual sexual encounters does not suffer the immediate psychological, physical, and emotional harm of the kind suffered by child sexual abuse victims. [According to Stephen F. Smith] "Far from being forced or enticed into submitting to sexual acts to be recorded in some fashion—the usual, incredibly harmful means through which child pornography is created—with self-produced child pornography, it is the minor who decides to create or distribute sexually explicit images of themselves." When the images are not coerced, the immediate and violent harm to a child that is the foundation of the child protection rationale is decidedly absent.

Even though self-produced images create a lasting permanent record that may cause future emotional and psychological harm to the minor, the circulation of such images does not "revictimize" the juvenile with every viewing. Without the underlying criminal and coercive methods of production, the circulation of self-produced images does not subject the minor to the same type of continued invasion and exploitation of his or her sexual autonomy and bodily integrity that is *so* degrading that it can only be characterized as a *continuation* of the act of sexual abuse. Although such images surely hold unlimited potential for subsequent harm if disseminated without the minor's consent, or even if the minor merely regrets having voluntarily distributed such images in the future, this harm is not *identical* or even substantially similar to the harm suffered by victims of child pornography. Like virtual pornography, the harm in sexting "does not necessarily follow from the speech, but depends upon some unquantified potential for subsequent criminal acts" [*Ashcroft v. Free Speech Coalition*, 2002]. This is not to discount the potential harm that follows from sexting. Certainly very real danger exists to minors engaging in sexting, and protecting minors from these potential harms may even justify regulation or prohibition of these images, but they are not the harm identified by the Supreme Court as the basis for a wholesale child pornography exemption from First Amendment protection.

It is important to note, however, that self-produced images, unlike virtual images, involve real children. Some of the language [in] *Ashcroft v. Free Speech Coalition* suggests the Court may be willing to include under its definition of child pornography images that harm children only through circulation. The relevant dicta referred to an unchallenged provision of the CPPA [Child Pornography Prevention Act] that prohibited the morphing of innocent pictures of real children so that an identifiable minor appears to be engaged in sexual activity. The Court noted that "[a]lthough morphed images may fall within the definition of virtual child pornography, they implicate the interests of real children and are in that sense closer to the images in *Ferber*" [*Ashcroft v. Free Speech Coalition*]. Even if a court finds that such morphed images are unprotected speech by way of the child pornography exception, as some lower courts have subsequently held, it does not automatically follow that self-produced images are necessarily also unprotected speech. Significantly, morphed images can be distinguished from self-produced images because they contain an element of exploitation and invasion of sexual autonomy that is absent from self-produced images. Furthermore, in the case of morphed images the law is being exercised purely in the favor of child victims, whereas in the case of self-produced images the children who appear in such images risk severe criminal penalties in exchange for "protection." . . .

Sexting cannot be excluded from First Amendment protection on the basis of the child pornography exception because it is not clear that the expressive interest in the sexted images is necessarily equivalent to that of child pornography. Although the Supreme Court held in [*New York v. Ferber*] that "[t]he value of permitting live performances and photographic reproductions of children engaged in lewd sexual conduct is exceedingly modest, if not *de minimis*," the Court later made clear that the judgment in *Ferber* was based on "how it was made, not on what it communicated" [*Ashcroft v. Free Speech*

Coalition]. In fact, the idea generally communicated by sexted images—teenage sexual activity—is, as the Supreme Court has recognized, a fact of modern life and has been a popular theme in art and literature throughout time. Any attempt to restrict the rights of minors to produce and distribute sexually explicit photographs of themselves must be weighted against the constitutional rights of minors to engage in such sexually expressive speech. Although minors are "persons" under the Constitution and are generally possessed of fundamental rights, a major question remains as to how and in what way these rights differ from the First Amendment rights of adults.

It Is Too Early to Legislate

Finding that sexting cannot be constitutionally prohibited as a form of child pornography does not require an abandonment of all efforts to regulate such conduct. Although a prohibition on sexting would not be narrowly tailored to serve the compelling interest of preventing the sexual abuse of children, the government is free to articulate new laws and punishments designed to protect minors from the harms particular to sexting. Such laws would be constitutional if they are narrowly tailored to a compelling government purpose or if the Supreme Court recognizes a new category of unprotected speech that encompasses all pornographic images of minors regardless of their relation to child sexual abuse. Furthermore, some sexting images may also be proscribed under existing statutes, to the extent that such images are obscene. Although obscenity regulations will not reach all sexting images, they would permit a ban on the most egregious, offensive, and potentially damaging images produced and circulated.

This preliminary inquiry into the problem of sexting leaves many important issues unaddressed. An appropriate response to juvenile self-production of pornographic images must balance the serious consequences of this conduct against the rights, if any, of adolescents to free sexual expression. Furthermore, it is essential that any response to the problem of sexting, whether penal or educational, should be consistent with existing legal and moral approaches to adolescent sexuality to avoid inconsistency and perverse consequences. As legislators, courts, prosecutors, parents, and educators develop responses to the problem of self-produced pornographic images, new and interesting questions must be answered. The phenomenon of sexting raises important issues such as the extent to which adolescent rights to free expression are congruent or dissimilar to the rights of adults and the extent to which the boundaries of pornography and obscenity are redefined by each generation. Addressing the problem of child pornography as a new and unique problem will avoid constitutional difficulties, prevent the application of overly harsh penalties to juvenile misadventure, and avoid undermining the legitimacy of traditional child pornography regulation.

> *"If teens are to be protected, they must be given the facts about homosexual behavior, not fantasies from the gay community."*

Schools Should Not Teach Positive Messages About Homosexuality

National Association for Research Therapy of Homosexuality

The National Association for Research Therapy of Homosexuality is a Christian-based organization. In the following viewpoint, the author cites a study conducted by sociologist Sander Breiner that proposed exposure to ideas about homosexuality has a significant impact on developing adolescent brains. According to Breiner, adolescence is a time filled with confusion about sexual identity—thus exposing teenagers to gay-affirming messages during these years may have a lasting impact. Teenagers who are exposed to homosexual messages by educators during an emotionally vulnerable time may, in Breiner's view, experience undue stress, depression, and damaged self-esteem, all of which can have an impact on brains.

As you read, consider the following questions:

1. According to this viewpoint, how does the teaching of gay-affirming ideas add to the problems teens already face?

2. What do the authors say is the impact of messages from teachers during adolescence, when teens are often undergoing significant neurological changes?

3. What does Sander Breiner say is the impact of homosexual indoctrination on prepubescent brain development?

Dr. Sander Breiner, a member of NARTH's [National Association for Research Therapy of Homosexuality] Scientific Advisory Committee, recently expanded upon a paper on "Adolescent Homosexuality" he presented at the November, 2004 NARTH conference in Washington, DC. (Dr. Breiner's paper is currently posted on the NARTH web site.)

Sexually questioning youth are vulnerable to the derailment of their normal heterosexuality, Dr. Breiner asserted, when they are urged to consider the possibility of being same-sex attracted.

Teen Brains Are Highly Susceptible

Dr. Breiner's paper dealt with the current scientific knowledge on the development of the brain during pre-teen and teen years as it relates to hormones and emotional maturity. One of the sources for this paper was a book edited by Dr. Ronald Dahl for the New York Academy of Sciences on Adolescent Neuroscience. Dr. Dahl is at the University of Pittsburgh and has written extensively on adolescent brain development.

Breiner noted that neuroscientists are convinced that the developing brain during the teen years is significantly influenced by external emotional and social factors. Stress factors, nutrition, and exercise can have an effect on the reproductive function that can lead to a suppression of ovarian and testicular functions. According to Breiner, "If the stress is chronic there can be a significant suppression of this reproductive axis."

Gay-Affirming Teachings Can Impact Brain Development

In an interview with NARTH's Editorial Director, Dr. Breiner notes that teens typically face stresses and confusion about their sexuality. Teaching gay-affirming ideas to teens can add to the problems they already face. The child who is taught that he or she may be homosexual can be stressful and may react in the following negative ways: hurt self esteem; poor body image; likelihood of depression; anxiety about how they will function socially; and a delayed response in functioning as a heterosexual, which makes their social skills even more limited. Gay-affirming materials "won't make someone homosexual, but certainly will contribute to problems in their development," said Breiner. "Adolescents have enough problems in establishing gender roles and this will increase these problems."

According to Breiner, this isn't simply a social or psychological threat to children but is a neurological problem as well. Actual brain changes take place. He notes that there is a strong connection between hormonal development and neurotransmitters that send messages for hormonal development. "If the wrong message gets sent, as is likely to occur when external messages are coming from teachers, then the child may experience a delay in proper sexual development."

Dr. Breiner observes that neuroscience studies are clear on this subject yet nothing has appeared yet in the psychiatric or psychological literature to deal with the connection between external gay-affirming messages and brain development.

"I am convinced that gay-affirming materials are injurious to children and will add to the psychological problems they already have as a normal part of development," said Breiner. "It is wrong to say that homosexuality is a viable alternative to heterosexuality. If teens are to be protected, they must be given the facts about homosexual behavior, not fantasies from the gay community."

In discussing the development of homosexuality in general, Dr. Breiner observed: "Human homosexuality is a symptom of some unresolved conflicts in a child's development psychologically. It is determined before the age of five, and usually between 1[frac12] to 3 years of age. If the individual has a neurosis, it was organized between ages 3 to 6. If they are of a borderline psychological organization, it was between ages 2 to 3. If they are psychotic, the psychological organization is under 2."

Educators Should Be Careful

In the conclusion to his paper on "Adolescent Homosexuality," Dr. Breiner observes:

> The brain that is developing (pre-puberty to adulthood), particularly in the area that deals with emotional and sexual development, is affected organically by social and physical stress. Homosexual indoctrination (direct or subtle), coercive or seductive can organically affect brain and sexual physiologic development to a modest or minimal degree. It cannot permanently produce homosexuality. However, it can certainly lead to a variety of difficulties commonly including hurt self-esteem, distortions in living, depression, selection of life goals, and other problems. Though the individual may eventually select a heterosexual life position, the preceding years of difficulties in developing and organizing one's life are likely to have more permanent deleterious effects. Therefore, any attitude by society and particularly educators that homosexuality is a reasonable or alternative lifestyle can significantly contribute to psychopathology in this vulnerable age.

> "When public schools only allow access to one side of an issue by blocking certain websites, they're engaging in illegal viewpoint discrimination."

Schools Should Allow Students Access to Information on Gay and Lesbian Issues

American Civil Liberties Union

The American Civil Liberties Union (ACLU) is a national organization that works to defend and preserve individual rights and liberties. In the following viewpoint, the ACLU takes issue with what it believes is the illegal use of web filtering software by Tennessee schools to prevent students from accessing online information about lesbian, gay, and transgender issues. In addition to denying students access to needed information for school projects and research, the ACLU believes that censorship of websites that contain information on gay and lesbian issues is discriminatory toward gay students and violates the law.

As you read, consider the following questions:

1. How does denying students access to content violate the law, according to the ACLU?

2. What is one problem identified by the ACLU regarding the web filtering software used by Tennessee schools?

3. How does the censorship software used by Tennessee schools engage the district in illegal viewpoint discrimination?

A s many as 107 Tennessee public school districts could be illegally preventing students from accessing online information about lesbian, gay, bisexual and transgender issues, according to a letter to sent to school officials by the American Civil Liberties Union [ACLU]. The letter demands that Knox County Schools, Metro Nashville Public Schools, and the Tennessee Schools Cooperative unblock the Internet filtering category designated "LGBT" [lesbian, gay, bisexual, transgender] so that students can access political and educational information about LGBT issues on school computers.

Suppressing Information Is Unacceptable

"When I found out about this web filtering software, I wasn't looking for anything sexual or inappropriate—I was looking for information about scholarships for LGBT students, and I couldn't get to it because of this software," said Andrew Emitt, a 17-year-old senior at Central High School in Knoxville. "Our schools shouldn't be keeping students in the dark about LGBT organizations and resources."

In its letter, the ACLU gives the districts and the Tennessee Schools Cooperative until April 29 [2009] to come up with a plan to restore access to the LGBT sites or any other category that blocks non-sexual websites advocating the fair treatment of LGBT people by the beginning of the 2009–2010 school year. If that deadline is not met, the ACLU will file a lawsuit.

"Students at Knox County and Metro Nashville schools are being denied access to content that is protected speech under the First Amendment as well as the Tennessee state constitution," said Tricia Herzfeld, Staff Attorney with the ACLU of Tennessee. "This kind of censorship does nothing but hurt students, whether they're being harassed at school and want to know about their legal rights or are just trying to finish an assignment for a class."

The Internet filtering software used by Knox County and Metro Nashville school districts blocks student access to the websites of many well-known national LGBT organizations, including:

- Parents, Families, and Friends of Lesbians and Gays (PFLAG)

- Gay, Lesbian and Straight Education Network (GLSEN)

- Human Rights Campaign (HRC)

- Marriage Equality USA

- Religious Coalition for the Freedom to Marry

- Gay and Lesbian Alliance Against Defamation (GLAAD)

- DignityUSA (an organization for LGBT Catholics)

In its demand letter, the ACLU notes that websites that urge LGBT persons to change their sexual orientation or gender identity through so-called "reparative therapy" or "ex-gay" ministries—a practice denounced as dangerous and harmful to young people by such groups as the American Psychological Association, the American Psychiatric Association, the American Medical Association, and the American Academy of Pediatrics—can still be easily accessed by students.

Tennessee Schools Discontinue Filters That Block Gay-Friendly Websites

[In May 2009, the ACLU] sued to challenge two Tennessee public school districts' policy of using certain Internet filtering software in their libraries. . . .

[In June 2009] the two Tennessee school districts at issue capitulated, and unblocked the pro-LGBT sites. Moreover, the change was made statewide across all Tennessee districts, and throughout Indiana, where the same ENA [Education Networks of America] filtering software is used.

Julie Hilden,
"Can a Public School's Library Block Pro-Gay Websites?
An ACLU Lawsuit Says No," FindLaw, June 5, 2009.

Information Is Biased

"One of the problems with this software is that it only allows students access to one side of information about topics that are part of the public debate right now, like marriage for same-sex couples," said Karyn Storts-Brinks, a librarian at Fulton High School in Knoxville, pointing out that the software blocks access to organizations that support marriage for same-sex couples like the Religious Coalition for Freedom to Marry or the Interfaith Working Group, while allowing access to organizations that oppose marriage equality. "Students who need to do research for assignments on current events can only get one viewpoint, keeping them from being able to cover both sides of the issue. That's not fair and can hinder their schoolwork."

"Public schools are supposed to be a place where students learn from the open exchange of ideas," said Eric Austin, a senior at Hume-Fogg High School in Nashville, which also uses the filtering software. "How are we supposed to be informed citizens and learn how to have respectful debate when our schools rule out an entire category of information for no good reason?"

No federal or state law requires school districts to block access to LGBT sites. Tennessee law, Tenn. Code § 49-1-221, only requires schools to implement filtering software to restrict information that is obscene or harmful to minors. About 80 percent of Tennessee public schools, including those in the Knox County and Metro Nashville districts, use filtering software provided by Education Networks of America (ENA), and the software's default setting blocks sites ENA categorizes as LGBT. The ACLU believes that most of the 107 Tennessee school districts that use ENA's filtering software keep the LGBT category blocked. ENA blocks access to a wide category of "LGBT" sites described on the organization's website as

> Sites that provide information regarding, support, promote, or cater to one's sexual orientation or gender identity including but not limited to lesbian, gay, bi-sexual, and transgender sites. This category does not include sites that are sexually gratuitous in nature which would typically fall under the Pornography category. Examples: glsen.org, gsanetwork.org, hrc.org.

"When public schools only allow access to one side of an issue by blocking certain websites, they're engaging in illegal viewpoint discrimination," said Hedy Weinberg, Executive Director of the ACLU of Tennessee. "Over a hundred other school districts in Tennessee use the same filtering software used in Metro Nashville and Knox County, and we're eager to find out whether any of those systems are also violating students' Constitutional rights by restricting access to LGBT sites."

> "Laws requiring parental notice or consent actually harm the young women they purport to protect by increasing the possibility of illegal and self-induced abortion, family violence, suicide, later abortions, and unwanted childbirth."

Abortion Parental Involvement Laws Are Harmful to Teens

NARAL Pro-Choice America

NARAL Pro-Choice America advocates pro-choice ideology in the area of reproductive rights. In the following viewpoint, NARAL argues that parental involvement laws, both ones that require parental notice and those that require parental consent before a minor can seek an abortion, are often harmful to teens. According to NARAL, many young women do turn to parents and other trusted adults in their lives before considering an abortion, but requiring parental consent and notification by law restricts minors' reproductive rights and in many cases endangers the physical and emotional health of young teens. Current judicial workarounds to parental consent and notification fail to protect the rights of minor patients, and in many cases, limit their ability to seek medical help and treatment.

As you read, consider the following questions:

1. According to this viewpoint, what are some of the main reasons young women hesitate to involve parents in their decision to have an abortion?

2. How do parental consent and notice laws endanger young women's health, in the view of the author?

3. According to the author, why are judicial-bypass procedures an inadequate alternative for young women seeking an abortion without parental consent and notification?

There are two types of parental-involvement laws: those that require parental *notice* and those that require parental *consent* before a minor can seek abortion services. Parental-notice laws require prior written notification of parents before an abortion can be performed, with limited exceptions, such as in cases of physical abuse, incest, or medical emergency. These laws also may prescribe other preconditions including a mandatory waiting period following the parents' receipt of notification, and/or judicial intervention if there are compelling reasons to avoid parental notification.

Parental-consent laws require that minors obtain the consent of one or both parents before they can receive abortion services. As is the case with parental notice, a judicial-bypass process is also generally included in parental-consent laws. The penalties for violating parental-consent laws range from civil liability and fines to imprisonment. The Supreme Court has ruled that parental-consent requirements are constitutional so long as they include a judicial-bypass procedure to accommodate those young women who cannot involve their parents.

Ideally, a teen facing a crisis will seek the advice and counsel of those who care for her most and know her best. In fact, even in the absence of laws mandating parental involvement, many young women do turn to their parents when they are considering abortion. Unfortunately, some young women cannot involve their parents because physical violence or emotional abuse is present in their homes, because their pregnancies are the result of incest, or because they fear parental anger and disappointment. Mandatory parental-involvement (consent and notice) laws do not solve the problem of inadequate family communication; they only exacerbate a potentially dangerous situation.

Current Law May Endanger Teens

In some circumstances, teens facing a crisis pregnancy feel compelled to travel to another state where there is a less stringent parental-involvement law or no such law at all, to avoid involving their parents and maintain their privacy. In the most dire of circumstances, some pregnant young women who fear telling their parents may resort to illegal or self-induced abortions that may result in death. Yet, despite these severe consequences, 37 states currently enforce laws that require a minor to obtain the consent of, or notify, an adult—typically a parent—prior to an abortion. And six other states have minors' access laws that are either enjoined or not enforced.

In recent years, Congress has considered two pieces of legislation to impose draconian criminal parental-involvement laws on every state in the country. The first, called the "Child Custody Protection Act" [CCPA], criminalizes caring and loving adults—including grandparents, adult siblings, and religious counselors—who accompany a teen out of state for abortion care if the home state parental-involvement law has not been met. The second, called the "Child Interstate Abortion Notification Act," would additionally impose an impossibly complex patchwork of parental-involvement laws on women and doctors across the country, in addition to the CCPA provisions, making it virtually impossible for young women to access abortion services in another state. Both measures would threaten young women's health and deny them the support and guidance they need from responsible and caring adults.

Government Cannot Mandate Healthy and Open Communication in Families

Government cannot mandate healthy family communication. Laws requiring parental notice or consent actually harm the young women they purport to protect by increasing the possibility of illegal and self-induced abortion, family violence, suicide, later abortions, and unwanted childbirth.

- A majority of young adults who are pregnant and seek abortion care indicate that their parents are aware that they are doing so. Furthermore, in states without parental-involvement laws, 61 percent of parents knew of their daughters' decision to terminate a pregnancy.

- The American Medical Association takes the position that: "Physicians should not feel or be compelled to require minors to involve their parents before deciding whether to undergo an abortion. . . . [M]inors should ultimately be allowed to decide whether parental involvement is appropriate."

- The American Academy of Pediatrics also opposes parental-involvement laws: "Legislation mandating parental involvement does not achieve the intended benefit of promoting family communication but it does increase the risk of harm to the adolescent by delaying access to appropriate medical care. . . . [M]inors should not be compelled or required to involve their parents in their decisions to obtain abortions, although they should be encouraged to discuss their pregnancies with their parents and other responsible adults."

- Parental-involvement laws appear to have had little effect on reducing abortion rates among teens.

Many Young Women Who Do Not Involve a Parent Have Good Reasons

Most young women find love, support, and safety in their home. Many, however, justifiably fear that they would be physically or emotionally abused if forced to disclose their pregnancy. Often, young women who do not involve a parent come from families where government-mandated disclosure would have devastating effects.

- An estimated 905,000 children were found to be victims of abuse or neglect in 2006. Young women considering abortion are particularly vulnerable because research shows that family violence is often at its worst during a family member's pregnancy.

- Nearly half of pregnant teens who have a history of abuse report being assaulted during their pregnancy, most often by a family member. As the Supreme Court has recognized, "Mere notification of pregnancy is frequently a flashpoint for battering and violence within the family. The number of battering incidents is high during the pregnancy and often the worst abuse can be associated with pregnancy."

- Among minors who did not tell a parent of their abortion, 30 percent had experienced violence in their family or feared violence or being forced to leave home. "My older sister got pregnant when she was seventeen. My mother pushed her against the wall, slapped her across the face and then grabbed her by the hair, pulled her through the living room out the front door and threw her off the porch. We don't know where she is now." [Helena Silverstein, quoting Melissa Jacobs].

- In Idaho, a 13-year-old student named Spring Adams was shot to death by her father after he learned she was to terminate a pregnancy caused by his acts of incest.

Mandatory Parental-Consent and Notice Laws Endanger Young Women's Health

Parental-consent and notice laws endanger young women's health by forcing some women—even some from healthy, loving families—to turn to illegal or self-induced abortion, to delay the procedure and increase the medical risk, or to bear a child against their will.

- In Indiana, Rebecca Bell, a young woman who had a very close relationship with her parents, died from an illegal abortion that she sought because she did not want her parents to know about her pregnancy. Indiana law required parental consent before she could have a legal abortion.

- The American Medical Association has noted that "[b]ecause the need for privacy may be compelling, minors may be driven to desperate measures to maintain the confidentiality of their pregnancies. They may run away from home, obtain a 'back alley' abortion, or resort to self-induced abortion. The desire to maintain secrecy has been one of the leading reasons for illegal abortion deaths since . . . 1973."

- Recognizing that maintaining confidentiality is essential to minors' willingness to obtain necessary health care related to sexual activity, all 50 states and the District of Columbia authorize minors to consent to the diagnosis and treatment of sexually transmitted infections without parental consent. Many states explicitly include testing and treatment of HIV, with only one state requiring parental notification if a minor tests positive for HIV. In addition, the Supreme Court has recognized that confidential access to contraceptives is essential for minors to exercise their constitutional right to privacy, and federal law requires confidentiality for minors receiving family-planning services through publicly funded programs, such as Title X and Medicaid.

- According to Leslie Tarr Laurie, president of Tapestry Health Systems, a Massachusetts-based health services provider: "Confidentiality is the cornerstone of our services. . . . We help teenagers avoid not only the costly and often tragic consequences of unintended pregnancy and childbearing, but also an early death from AIDS. The bottom line is, if we don't assure access to confidential health care, teenagers simply will stop seeking the care they desire and need."

- The American Medical Association concluded in a 1992 study that parental-consent and notice laws "increase the gestational age at which the induced pregnancy termination occurs, thereby also increasing the risk associated with the procedure." Although a first or second trimester abortion is far safer than childbirth, the risk of complications significantly increases for each week that elapses after eight weeks.

Judicial-Bypass Provisions Fail to Protect Young Women

In challenges to two different parental-involvement laws, the Supreme Court has stated that a state statute requiring parental involvement must have some sort of bypass procedure, such as a judicial bypass, in order to be constitutional. No one person may have an absolute veto over a minor's decision to have an abortion. Thus, most states that require parental consent or notice provide—at least as a matter of law—a judicial bypass through which a young woman can seek a court order allowing an abortion without parental involvement.

But bypass procedures are often an inadequate alternative for young women, especially when courts are either not equipped or resistant to granting judicial bypasses. For adults, going to court for a judicial order is difficult. For young women without a lawyer, it is overwhelming and at times impossible. Some young women cannot maneuver the legal procedures required or cannot attend hearings scheduled during school hours. Others do not go or delay going because they fear that the proceedings are not confidential or that they will be recognized by people at the courthouse. Many experience fear and distress and do not want to reveal intimate details of their personal lives to strangers. The time required to schedule the court proceeding may result in a delay of a week or more, thereby increasing the health risks of the abortion. And in many instances, courts are not equipped to handle bypass proceedings in accord with constitutional regulations. Worse yet, some young women who do manage to arrange a hearing face judges who are vehemently anti-choice and who routinely deny petitions of minors who show that they are mature or that the bypass is in their best interest, despite rulings by the U.S. Supreme Court that the bypass must be granted in those circumstances.

- In denying the petition of one young woman, a Missouri judge stated: "Depending upon what ruling I make I hold in my hands the power to kill an unborn child. In our society it's a lot easier to kill an unborn child than the most vicious murderer. . . . I don't believe that this particular juvenile has sufficient intellectual capacity to make a determination that she is willing to kill her own child."

- A Toledo, Ohio judge denied a bypass for a 17-year-old, an "A" student who planned to attend college and who testified she was not financially or emotionally prepared for college and motherhood at the same time, stating that the girl had "not had enough hard knocks in her life."

- In Louisiana, a judge denied a 15-year-old a bypass petition after asking her a series of inappropriate questions, including what the minor would say to the fetus about her decision. Her request was granted only after a rehearing by six appellate court judges.

- A Pennsylvania study found that of the 60 judicial districts in the state, only eight were able to provide complete information about Pennsylvania's judicial-bypass procedure. Some county courts referred minors to anti-choice crisis pregnancy centers that typically provide false and misleading information about abortion and pressure women to carry their pregnancies to term.

- The Alabama Supreme Court upheld a trial court's denial of a petition for a 17-year-old because the minor's testimony appeared "rehearsed" and she did not show "any emotion." The trial court refused to find that the minor was mature and well-informed enough to make her own decision or that an abortion was in her best interests—despite the fact that the 17-year-old high school senior had a 3.0 grade point average, had been accepted to college, had discussed her options with the father of the fetus, had spoken to a doctor, a counselor, her godmother, and her 20-year-old sister, was able to describe the abortion procedure, was informed about its risks, and had testified that her legal guardian had thrown a teenage relative out of the house when she became pregnant.

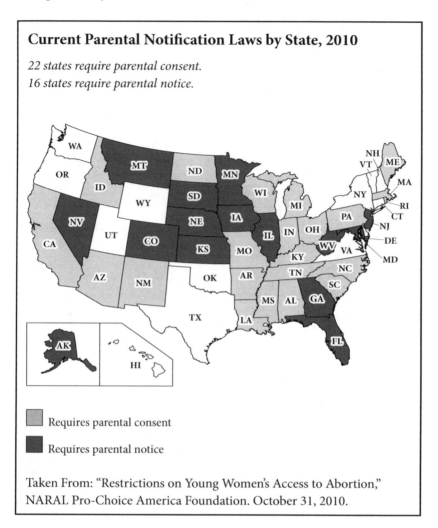

Current Parental Notification Laws by State, 2010

22 states require parental consent.
16 states require parental notice.

Requires parental consent

Requires parental notice

Taken From: "Restrictions on Young Women's Access to Abortion,"
NARAL Pro-Choice America Foundation. October 31, 2010.

The Effects of Teenage Childbearing Can Be Devastating

The forced childbearing among teenagers that can result from parental-consent and notice laws can have devastating effects on the health and life chances of young women and their children.

- Approximately one-third of American women become pregnant before the age of 20.

- Teenage girls are more than 24 times more likely to die from childbirth than from first trimester legal abortions.

- Fewer than 60 percent of teen mothers graduate from high school by age 25—compared to 90 percent of those who postpone childbearing. Additionally, among African-American and Hispanic teens, those who postpone childbearing until age 20 are more likely to complete some college education.

- Twenty-five percent of teen mothers live below the federal poverty line. Nearly 80 percent of teen mothers eventually go on welfare. Teens that give birth also spend a greater length of time receiving public assistance—an average of three years longer than older mothers through age 35. Teen mothers are also more likely to have lower family incomes later in life.

- Infants of teen mothers are one-third more likely to suffer from low birthweight (less than 5.5 pounds) than those born to older mothers. The children of teenage parents have an increased risk of abuse and neglect and are more likely to become teenage parents themselves, thus perpetuating the cycle of poverty.

An Emphasis Should Be Placed on Reducing Teen Pregnancy

Abortion among teenagers should be made less necessary, not more difficult and dangerous. A comprehensive approach to promoting adolescent reproductive health and reducing teen pregnancy will require an array of components, including:

- age-appropriate health and sex education with medically accurate information;

- access to confidential health services, including family planning;

- life-options programs that offer teens practical life skills and the motivation to delay sexual activity; and

- programs for pregnant and parenting teens that teach parenting skills and help ensure that teens finish school.

Such an approach has never been implemented on a significant scale in the United States, and several studies of specific HIV-prevention and sex education programs demonstrate positive outcomes such as increased knowledge, delay in onset of sex, reduction in the frequency of sex, or increased contraceptive use. The wisest policy gives teenagers the tools they need to avoid pregnancy and forsakes misguided efforts to insert the government into delicate family situations.

| "Well designed parental-involvement laws have been surprisingly effective at reducing abortion rates among minors."

Abortion Parental Involvement Laws Reduce Abortion Rates

Michael J. New

Michael J. New is an assistant professor of political science at the University of Alabama and has worked for the Family Research Council and the Witherspoon Institute. In the following viewpoint, New urges pro-life advocates to pressure political candidates to pass parental-involvement laws. New considers parental notification and parental consent laws as viable tools to help reduce the number of abortions sought by minors, citing various studies as proof that parental notification laws effectively reduce the number of abortions among teens. He asserts that parental consent laws, especially, those requiring the consent of both parents, are especially effective.

As you read, consider the following questions:

1. According to the author, how do parental notification laws impact abortion rates among minors?

2. Why are parental consent laws more effective than parental notice laws, in the author's view?

3. What federal legislation has been introduced that would considerably strengthen state-level parental involvement laws?

Political candidates who support legal abortion have been changing their rhetoric in recent years. Indeed, during the current election cycle [2008], a number of pro-choice candidates, including Barack Obama, have expressed an interest in lowering the incidence of abortion. Such statements present a unique opportunity for the pro-life movement. Indeed, pro-lifers should insist that these candidates support pro-life parental-involvement laws. Such laws enjoy broad support and unlike other laws limiting abortion, they can be easily justified as a parental-rights issue. Furthermore, my recent study for the Family Research Council provides evidence that well designed parental-involvement laws have been surprisingly effective at reducing abortion rates among minors.

Parental-Involvement Laws Are Effective

Indeed, there are a number of academic and policy studies, which demonstrate the effectiveness of pro-life parental-involvement laws. Four studies in peer-reviewed academic journals use time-series, cross-sectional data to simultaneously analyze all the enacted pro-life parental-involvement laws over an extended period of time. These studies find that these pieces of legislation reduce the in-state minor abortion rate by anywhere from 13 to 19 percent. Case studies of parental-involvement laws that have been enacted in Massachusetts, Indiana, Missouri, and Minnesota arrive at similar conclusions about the effects of parental-involvement laws.

However, the best case study of a pro-life parental-involvement law appeared in *The New England Journal of Medicine* in 2006. This study analyzed the Texas parental-notification law that took effect in 2000. The authors found that the law resulted in statistically significant declines in the abortion rate in Texas among 15-year-olds, 16-year-olds, and 17-year-olds. Now the authors did find some evidence that some 17-year-olds were able to circumvent the law by waiting until their 18th birthday to have an abortion. However, they found little evidence that Texas minors were circumventing the law by obtaining abortions in neighboring states.

My recently released Family Research Council study contributes to this body of research. It is actually the first study that compares the effect of different types of pro-life parental-involvement legislation. The results indicate that parental-involvement laws reduce the minor abortion rate by 13 percent—a finding that is consistent with other research on the subject. However, state laws that require parental consent instead of parental notification are even more effective, reducing the abortion rate by an average of 19 percent. This finding held true for all age groups that were analyzed—17-year-olds, 16-year-olds, and 15-year-olds.

Parental Consent Laws Are Particularly Effective

There are a number of reasons why parental-consent laws might be more effective than parental-notice laws. Consent laws, unlike notification laws, would effectively give parents the ability to prevent an abortion from being performed on their daughter. Additionally, a parental-notice law might not deter a minor who feels she can intercept the notification. Finally, it should also be noted that abortion providers might have a greater incentive to follow parental-consent laws. A missed notification can possibly be blamed on timing or other incidental factors. However, failure to obtain consent would likely be seen as the responsibility of the abortion provider and could result in legal action—especially if the parents did not approve of the abortion being performed.

Interestingly, those parental-involvement laws that require the involvement of two parents instead of one are even more effective. The regression model indicates that these laws reduce the minor abortion rate by 31 percent. Now only three states—Minnesota, Mississippi, and North Dakota—have enacted parental-involvement laws that require the involvement of two parents. However, the substantial abortion declines that have occurred in each of these states suggest that they are models that other states should follow.

These abortion declines all sound impressive. However, it is entirely possible that some of these in-state abortion reductions could be offset by minors who obtain abortions in neighboring states where the laws are more permissive. Federal legislation has been introduced that would considerably strengthen these state-level parental-involvement laws. The Child Custody Protection Act that has been introduced in the

U.S. Senate and the Child Interstate Abortion Notification Act (CIANA) that has been introduced in the U.S. House would make it a felony for anyone other than a parent to take a child across state lines for the purpose of obtaining an abortion.

CIANA and the Child Custody Protection Act passed the House and Senate respectively in 2006. However, this legislation ultimately was defeated when Senate Democrats refused to appoint members to a conference committee to work out the differences in the two pieces of legislation. Regardless, by making it more difficult for a minor to obtain an abortion in neighboring states, these federal laws could considerably strengthen the state-level parental-involvement laws that are already in place. Indeed, both CIANA and the Child Custody Protection Act should both remain a high priority for pro-life organizations working on federal legislation.

Pro-Life Supporters Should Support Pro-Life Legislation

Meanwhile at the state level, the pro-life movement still has plenty of work to do. Right now [2008] about 36 states have pro-life parental-involvement laws in effect. However, about 15 of these laws only require parental notification. Furthermore, only three of these laws mandate the involvement of two parents. Strengthening these state laws could be a worthwhile project for pro-life activists. The Supreme Court has consistently upheld strong state-level parental-involvement laws, and it is certainly possible that other legislative proposals to limit abortion at the state level may not withstand judicial scrutiny.

During the 2008 election campaign, abortion will undoubtedly continue to be a major issue. The Supreme Court appointments by the next president will likely determine the extent to which federal government and the states are able to protect unborn children. It is laudable that a number of candidates have expressed an interest in lowering the incidence of abortion. However, serious pro-life voters should support only those candidates who have a consistent track record of supporting pro-life legislation. While campaign rhetoric often does not amount to much, this study—and other studies—provide solid evidence that well designed laws are effective at protecting mothers and their unborn children.

Periodical and Internet Sources Bibliography

The following articles have been selected to supplement the diverse views presented in this chapter.

Mike Celizic	"Teen 'Sexting': Youthful Prank or Sex Crime?" *Today*, March 10, 2009. http://today.msnbc.msn.com.
Amanda Dennis, Stanley K. Henshaw, Theodore J. Joyce, Lawrence B. Finer, and Kelly Blanchard	"The Impact of Laws Requiring Parental Involvement for Abortion: A Literature Review," *Guttmacher Policy Review*, March 2009.
Lisa Falkenberg	"Study: Texas Parental Law Might Lower—and Delay—Teen Abortion," *Houston Chronicle*, March 9, 2006.
Julie Hilden	"How Should Teens' 'Sexting'—the Sending of Revealing Photos—Be Regulated?" Findlaw's Writ, April 28, 2009. http://writ.news.findlaw.com.
Sameer Hinduja and Justin W. Patchin	"Sexting: A Brief Guide for Educators and Parents," Cyberbullying Research Center, 2010. www.cyberbullying.us.
Richard Kim	"Against 'Bullying' or On Loving Queer Kids," *The Nation*, October 6, 2010.
Larry Magid	"Teen Sexting: Troubling but Don't Overreact," October 29, 2010. www.education.com.
Paula Parker-Sawyer	"Teen Pregnancy in the Courtroom," *Policy & Practice*, October 1, 2009.
Matthew S. Robinson	"Scared Not to Be Straight: Harassment of LGBT Teens Prompts Anti-bullying Initiatives," Edutopia, October 29, 2010. www.edutopia.org.

For Further Discussion

Chapter 1

1. Several factors influence teen attitudes toward sexuality, including parents, peers, religion, media, and public personalities. Which do you consider to be the most important and influential role models discussed in the viewpoints in this chapter, particularly in terms of teenage attitudes and behaviors regarding sex, and why?

2. Teenagers have access to information from a variety of media sources, including television and the Internet. Michael Rich states that media influence significantly impacts teenage attitudes toward sexual initiation, while Laurence Steinberg and Kathryn C. Monahan state that media influence on teenage sexuality is exaggerated. What reasons does each give to support their positions? Who do you agree with, and why?

Chapter 2

1. Communication between parents and teens has improved significantly in many areas, but most teens are still uncomfortable discussing issues surrounding sexual health with their parents. Nicholas Lagina and Alicia Whittaker write that parent-teen communication about sexual issues is necessary to help teens make wise decisions about sex. Do you agree or disagree? Why?

2. The National Campaign to Prevent Teen and Unplanned Pregnancy regards teen pregnancy as a significant problem that results in many negative outcomes for both teen parents and their babies. However, Amelia Gentleman cites research that views teen pregnancy as an opportunity, al-

lowing teen parents to increase achievement and motivation. Which viewpoint do you agree with, and why?

3. Teen dating violence is an important aspect of adolescent romantic relationships, but Carrie Mulford and Peggy C. Giordano state that this problem is not adequately understood because current research fails to examine this issue outside the context of adult relationships. What are some major differences between violent behaviors associated with teen relationships versus adult relationships?

Chapter 3

1. The decision to increase funding of abstinence education programs in schools set off a nationwide debate about the best way to educate teens regarding sex. Christine C. Kim and Robert Rector argue that abstinence-based sex education programs have proven to be successful, but Heather D. Boonstra cites several examples in which abstinence-based education has failed to help teens. Who do you agree with, and why? What, in your opinion, is the best way to educate teens about sex?

2. The conflict about sex education often focuses on the difference between those who believe that sex education is a matter best left to parents and those who advocate for comprehensive sex education in schools and other community settings. Do you think that families and parents are the best and most effective setting for discussions about sex? Why, or why not?

Chapter 4

1. Sexting is an increasingly popular phenomenon among young people, many of whom do not realize the legal implications of sexting, which can currently be prosecuted as a pornographic offense. Sarah Wastler outlines the inability of current law to address this problem, and notes that the laws need to be changed to better accommodate sex-

ting. Do you agree with her? Explain your reasons, citing specific examples in support of your argument.

2. Several states currently have parental notification and parental consent laws in place, limiting a minor's right to seek an abortion without prior consent of her parents or legal guardians. NARAL argues that these laws often place teens at risk, while Michael J. New writes that these laws help reduce abortions. Do you agree that parental notification laws are needed? Explain why.

Organizations to Contact

The editors have compiled the following list of organizations concerned with the issues debated in this book. The descriptions are derived from materials provided by the organizations. All have publications or information available for interested readers. The list was compiled on the date of publication of the present volume; names, addresses, phone and fax numbers, and e-mail and Internet addresses may change. Be aware that many organizations take several weeks or longer to respond to inquiries, so allow as much time as possible.

Advocates for Youth
2000 M Street NW, Suite 750, Washington, DC   20036
(202) 419-3420 • fax: (202) 419-1448
e-mail: info@advocatesforyouth.org
website: www.advocatesforyouth.org

Advocates for Youth is a national organization that champions efforts to help young people make informed and responsible decisions about their reproductive and sexual health. The organization believes in promoting a realistic approach to adolescent sexual health and information, focusing its efforts on young people between the ages of fourteen and twenty-five in the United States and around the world. Its website includes numerous publications on adolescent reproductive and sexual health, sex education, and adolescent sexual behavior.

Coalition for Positive Sexuality (CPS)
3712 N. Broadway, PMB #191, Chicago, IL   60613
(773) 604-1654
website: www.positive.org

The Coalition for Positive Sexuality (CPS) is a grassroots, direct-action group originally founded in 1992 by a group of Chicago high-school students. Funded through donations and grants, CPS aims to provide teens with candid sex education materials in order to encourage informed decisions about sex and help facilitate dialogue in public schools on condom availability and sex education. CPS publishes the pamphlet *Just Say Yes*, which provides information on resources for victims of violence and HIV testing.

Family Research Council (FRC)

801 G Street NW, Washington, DC   20001
(202) 393-2100 • fax: (202) 393-2134
e-mail: corrdept@frc.org
website: www.frc.org

The Family Research Council (FRC) is a nonprofit organization that aims to advance faith, family, and freedom in public policy and the media via research and public education. FRC reviews legislation, meets with policy makers, and publishes books and pamphlets to maintain a presence in print and broadcast media. It also offers outreach services for pastors and churches to help advance their ideas about marriage and family as the foundation of a civil society. The FRC website includes articles on human sexuality, abstinence and sexual health, and links to several videos and presentations on pregnancy and sexually transmitted diseases geared toward young adults.

Focus on the Family

Colorado Springs, CO   80995
(800) 232-6459 • fax: (719) 531-3424
e-mail: help@focusonthefamily.com
website: http://focusonthefamily.com

Focus on the Family is an organization that promotes Christian values and strong family ties. It identifies itself as a global Christian ministry that provides help and resources for parents to raise their children according to biblical principles. The parenting portion of the Focus on the Family website has sections devoted to sexuality and teens that include resources for both teens and parents, including several articles and fact sheets.

Gay, Lesbian, and Straight Education Network (GLSEN)
90 Broad Street, 2nd Floor, New York, NY   10004
(212) 727-0135 • fax: (212) 727-0254
e-mail: glsen@glsen.org
website: www.glsen.org

The Gay, Lesbian, and Straight Education Network (GLSEN) is a national organization that works to ensure safe schools for all students regardless of sexual orientation or gender identity/ expression. GLSEN believes that homophobia and heterosexism undermine healthy school cultures, and the organization works to educate teachers, students, and the public about the negative effects of sexual bias. GLSEN sponsors several websites, including THINKB4YOUSPEAK, which raises awareness about anti-LGBT (lesbian, gay, bisexual, transgender) language, and provides research and information on gay and lesbian issues to students, parents, and teachers in order to combat anti-gay bias and hate-motivated violence in schools through education.

Guttmacher Institute
1301 Connecticut Ave. NW, Suite 700, Washington, DC   20036
(202) 296-4012 • fax: (202) 223-5756
e-mail: info@guttmacher.org
website: www.guttmacher.org

The Guttmacher Institute is a nonprofit organization devoted to advancing sexual and reproductive health in the United States and across the world via a multilayered approach that includes research, policy analysis, and education. Among the institute's resources are several publications related to sexual and reproductive health, including *International Perspectives on Sexual and Reproductive Health* and the *Guttmacher Policy Review.*

Healthy Teen Network
1501 Saint Paul Street, Suite 124, Baltimore, MD   21202
(410) 685-0410 • fax: (410) 685-0481
website: www.healthyteennetwork.org

Healthy Teen Network is a national organization that focuses on adolescent health and well-being with an emphasis on teen pregnancy prevention, teen pregnancy, and related parenting issues. Healthy Teen Network promotes comprehensive and coordinated services among professionals and organizations through education, advocacy, and networking. The goal is to provide adolescents and teen parents access to the services and information they need to help make responsible childbearing and family formation decisions. The website also includes links to several articles on teen-related health issues and fact sheets on such topics as contraception, sexually transmitted diseases, abstinence programs, and LGBT-specific health issues.

The Heritage Foundation

214 Massachusetts Ave. NE, Washington, DC   20002
(202) 546-4400
e-mail: info@heritage.org
website: http://heritage.org

The Heritage Foundation is a public policy research institute that supports the ideas of limited government and the free-market system. It promotes the view that the welfare system has contributed to the problems of illegitimacy and teenage pregnancy. Among the foundation's numerous publications is its *Backgrounder* series and the Heritage Foundation blog, titled *The Foundry*, both of which include articles on teenage pregnancy, abstinence education, and teenage sexuality.

It Gets Better Project

8315 Beverly Blvd., Suite 101, Los Angeles, CA   90048
e-mail: info@itgetsbetter.org
website: www.itgetsbetter.org

The It Gets Better Project was established in 2010 with the goal of inspiring hope for young people facing harassment. The website for the initiative includes hundreds of videos and stories uploaded by celebrities, organizations, newsmakers, and young people. These resources aim to provide young people who are lesbian, gay, bisexual, or transgender with a place to access inspirational stories, watch videos, and seek help, all with a goal of reducing and preventing teen suicide.

Love Is Respect
PO Box 16180, Austin, TX   78716
(866) 331-9474 • fax: (512) 794-1199
e-mail: media@loveisrespect.org
website: www.loveisrespect.org

Love Is Respect is a national teen dating abuse hotline and website that provides resources for teens, parents, friends, peer advocates, government officials, and the general public. Launched in 2007 with help from founding corporate sponsor Liz Claiborne, Love Is Respect provides 24-hour resources both online and via the phone. Its counselors are trained to offer support, information, and advocacy for those involved in dating abuse relationships. The website for the organization includes several informational resources and fact sheets for young people, including *Dating Abuse Fast Facts, Breaking Up,* and *Support for a Friend,* as well as surveys to help teens determine if they are in an abusive relationship.

The National Campaign to Prevent Teen and Unplanned Pregnancy
1776 Massachusetts Ave. NW, Suite 200
Washington, DC   20036
(202) 478-8500 • fax: (202) 478-8588
website: www.thenationalcampaign.org

The National Campaign to Prevent Teen and Unplanned Pregnancy is a nonprofit, nonpartisan organization founded in 1996 with the goal of reducing the teen pregnancy rate in the United States by one-third between 1996 and 2005. Since the nation achieved this goal, in 2006 the National Campaign set a new goal—this time to reduce teen pregnancy rate by another one-third by 2015. Additionally, the organization expanded its focus on preventing teen pregnancy to also reduce unplanned pregnancy among young adults. The National

Campaign advocates prevention of teen pregnancy by supporting a combination of responsible values and policies in the public and private sectors and by encouraging similar responsible choices among teens and young adults. In addition to sponsoring several pregnancy and birth control information websites such as sexreally.com and StayTeen.org, the National Campaign publishes an annual survey of adults and teens on the issues surrounding teen pregnancy titled *With One Voice.*

Planned Parenthood Federation of America

434 West 33rd Street, New York, NY   10001
(212) 541-7800 • fax: (212) 245-1845
website: www.plannedparenthood.org

Founded in 1916, Planned Parenthood is the world's largest and oldest voluntary family planning organization. Planned Parenthood believes that every individual has a fundamental right to decide when or whether to have a child, and that every child should be wanted and loved. Planned Parenthood advocates access to comprehensive sex education and reproductive choice. It publishes information on sexuality, sexual orientation and gender, and sexually transmitted diseases on its website and also includes a section that provides parents with tools and a list of resources to help initiate conversations about sex with their teens.

Respect, Inc.

212 Hamilton Ave., Frankfort, IL   60423
(877) 673-7732 • fax: (414) 258-4858
website: www.sexrespect.com

Respect, Inc., is the organization that developed "Sex Respect," a sex education curriculum that stresses abstinence among teens. The curriculum teaches youths that abstaining from premarital sex is their right, is in society's best interest, and is in the spirit of true sexual freedom. The website provides several informational materials on abstinence, including a brochure titled *Love and Life: A Christian Sexual Morality Guide for Teens* as well as the "Love and Life Program," an abstinence-based sex education curriculum geared toward parents and teachers of middle school and high school children.

Sex, Etc.

Center for Applied Psychology, Rutgers University
41 Gordon Road, Suite C, Piscataway, NJ   08854
(732) 445-7929 • fax: (732) 445-5333
e-mail: answered@rci.rutgers.edu
website: www.sexetc.org

Sex, Etc. is an award-winning, teen-produced website and newsletter sponsored by Answer, a youth-driven sexuality education initiative, which answers questions from teens to provide sexual health information. Written and produced by teens for teens, the *Sex, Etc.* magazine, which is available online, talks about love, sex, abstinence, contraception, pregnancy, and other topics.

Sexuality Information and Education Council of the United States (SIECUS)

1706 R Street, Washington, DC   20009
(202) 265-2405 • fax: (202) 462-2340
website: www.siecus.org

The Sexuality Information and Education Council of the United States (SIECUS) is an organization of educators, physicians, social workers, and others who support the individual's right to acquire knowledge of sexuality and who encourage responsible sexual behavior. The council promotes comprehensive sex education for all children that includes AIDS education, teaching about homosexuality, and instruction about contraceptives and sexually transmitted diseases. Its publications include fact sheets, annotated bibliographies by topic, the booklet *Talk About Sex*, and the monthly SIECUS Report.

Teen-Aid

723 E. Jackson, Spokane, WA   99207
(509) 482-2868
website: www.teen-aid.org

Teen-Aid is an international nonprofit organization founded in 1981 with the purpose of reducing premarital sexual activity. The organization promotes traditional family values and sexual morality via media presentations and provides teaching resources, including publishing a public school sex education curriculum. The website also includes several articles on abstinence and abstinence research.

Bibliography of Books

Bill Albert | *With One Voice 2010: America's Adults and Teens Sound Off About Teen Pregnancy.* The National Campaign to Prevent Teen and Unplanned Pregnancy: Washington, DC: December 2010.

Louisa Allen | *Young People and Sexuality Education: Rethinking Key Debates.* New York: Palgrave Macmillan, 2011.

Stephen Arterburn, Fred Stoeker, and Mike Yorkey | *Preparing Your Son for Every Man's Battle: Honest Conversations About Sexual Integrity.* Colorado Springs, CO: WaterBrook Press, 2010.

Judith K. Balswick and Jack O. Balswick | *Authentic Human Sexuality: An Integrated Christian Approach.* Downers Grove, IL: InterVarsity Press, 2008.

Kathy Belge and Mark Bieschke | *Queer: The Ultimate LGBT Guide for Teens.* San Francisco, CA: Zest Books, 2011.

Dennis Carlson and Donyell Roseboro, eds. | *The Sexuality Curriculum and Youth Culture.* New York: Peter Lang, 2011.

Heather Corinna | *S.E.X. The All-You-Need-to-Know Progressive Sexuality Guide to Get You Through High School and College.* New York: Marlowe, 2007.

Alesha E. Doan and Jean Calterone Williams	*The Politics of Virginity: Abstinence in Sex Education*. New York: Praeger, 2008.
M. Gigi Durham	*The Lolita Effect: The Media Sexualization of Young Girls and What We Can Do About It.* Woodstock, NY: Overlook Press, 2009.
Naomi B. Farber	*Adolescent Pregnancy: Policy and Prevention Services*. New York: Springer, 2009.
Jessica Fields	*Risky Lessons: Sex Education and Social Inequality*. Newark, NJ: Rutgers University Press, 2008.
Heather Godsey and Lara Blackwood Pickrel, eds.	*Oh God, Oh God, Oh God!: Young Adults Speak Out About Sexuality and Christian Spirituality*. St. Louis, MO: Chalice Press, 2010.
Miriam Grossman	*You're Teaching My Child What? A Physician Exposes the Lies of Sex Education and How They Harm Your Child*. Washington, DC: Regnery, 2009.
Richard Guerry	*Public and Permanent: The Golden Rule of the 21st Century*. Bloomington, IN: Balboa Press, 2011.
Nikol Hassler	*Sex: A Book for Teens*. San Francisco, CA: Zest Books, 2010.

Elizabeth Henderson
100 Questions You'd Never Ask Your Parents. Richmond, VA: Uppman, 2007.

Thomas A. Jacobs
Teens Take It to Court: Young People Who Challenged the Law and Changed Your Life. Minneapolis, MN: Free Spirit, 2006.

Fred Kaeser
What Your Child Needs to Know About Sex: A Parents' Guide to Early, Open, and Effective Communication. Berkeley, CA: Celestian Arts, 2011.

Diane E. Levin and Jean Kilbourne
So Sexy So Soon: The New Sexualized Childhood and What Parents Can Do to Protect Their Kids. New York: Ballantine Books, 2008.

Kristin Luker
When Sex Goes to School: Warring Views on Sex—and Sex Education—Since the Sixties. New York: W.W. Norton, 2006.

Maureen E. Lyon and Lawrence J. D'Angelo
Teenagers, HIV, and AIDS: Insights from Youths Living with the Virus. Westport, CT: Praeger, 2006.

Mike A. Males
Teenage Sex and Pregnancy: Modern Myths, Unsexy Realities. Santa Barbara, CA: Praeger/ABC-CLIO, 2010.

Sharon Maxwell
The Talk: A Breakthrough Guide to Raising Healthy Kids in an Oversexualized, Online, In-Your-Face World. New York: Penguin, 2008.

Joe S. McIlhaney, Jr. and Freda McKissic Bush	*Hooked: New Science on How Casual Sex Is Affecting Our Children.* Chicago, IL: Northfield, 2008.
C.J. Pascoe	*Dude, You're a Fag: Masculinity and Sexuality in High School.* Berkeley, CA: University of California Press, 2007.
Helena Silverstein	*Girls on the Stand: How Courts Fail Pregnant Minors.* New York: New York University Press, 2007.
Rae Simons	*Teen Parents.* Philadelphia, PA: Mason Crest, 2010.
Jessica Valenti	*The Purity Myth: How America's Obsession with Virginity Is Hurting Young Women.* Berkeley, CA: Seal Press, 2010.
Ellin Stebbins Waldal	*Tornado Warning: A Memoir of Teen Dating Violence and Its Effect on a Woman's Life.* Encinitas, CA: Sound Beach, 2011.
Arlene M. Weisz and Beverly M. Black	*Programs to Reduce Teen Dating Violence and Sexual Assault: Perspectives on What Works.* New York: Columbia University Press, 2009.
Unni Wikan	*In Honor of Fadime: Murder and Shame.* Chicago: University of Chicago Press, 2008.

Index